WILLIAM MARSH RICE

The above portrait by an unknown artist shows Rice in middle age. One copy of the original hangs in the Founder's Room, Rice University, another in the Rice-Cherry House.

William Marsh Rice and His Institute

A Biographical Study

Edited by Sylvia Stallings Morris

From the papers and research notes of

Andrew Forest Muir

Rice University Studies

Houston, Texas

FOREWORD

For a number of years prior to his death in 1969, Professor Andrew Forest Muir was engaged in collecting the material to write an account of the life of William Marsh Rice, founder of the Rice Institute, now called Rice University. To this end, Professor Muir received a fellowship from the Guggenheim Foundation which allowed him to take the time to consult in detail the courthouse records of Harris and its neighboring counties, where many of William Marsh Rice's financial transactions were recorded, as well as providing him with an opportunity to visit and consult records in Springfield, Massachusetts, where Rice was born and spent his early years, in Dunellen, New Jersey, where Rice and his wife kept a country estate for some years, and in New York City, where Rice spent the last years of his life.

On the basis of the material that he collected, Professor Muir wrote and published a number of short articles on special aspects of William Marsh Rice's life and career. The most important of these articles are "William Marsh Rice, Houstonian," *East Texas Historical Journal,* II, 1 (Feb., 1964), pp. 32-39 and "Murder on Madison Avenue: The Rice Case Revisited," *Southwest Review* (Winter, 1959), pp. 1-9. In addition, at the time of his death, Professor Muir left a number of unpublished manuscripts, several of which had been read before one or another of the local historical societies but which had never been revised for publication and several of which were no more than preliminary sketches. The most significant of these unfinished papers are "William Marsh Rice and his Institute," "William Marsh Rice, His Life and Death," "The Beginnings of the Rice Institute," "William Marsh Rice, His Life and Death, the

History of a Fortune," and "A Man Morbidly Virtuous—Albert T. Patrick," the manuscripts of all of which are now found with the Andrew Forest Muir Papers that have been placed in the Archives of the Fondren Library at Rice University.

Professor Muir, however, never found the opportunity to bring his work together and to utilize the vast amounts of detailed information that he had collected concerning William Marsh Rice. That these materials have now been organized and edited is due to the dedicated interest of Professor Muir's executors, the late Charles W. Hamilton and his wife Mary Alice Hamilton, the encouragement of Willoughby Williams and Ben Blanton of the Development Office of Rice University, and the support of a number of friends of Rice who contributed generously toward financing the project.

For the actual work of sorting through Professor Muir's papers, checking his sources, filling in the gaps, and bringing life to inanimate data, *Rice University Studies* has had the extremely good fortune to secure the services of Sylvia Stallings Morris (BA, Bryn Mawr College, 1948). Mrs. Morris has produced the following study of William Marsh Rice. It is not intended to replace the work that Professor Muir, with his love of minute detail and his insistence on exhaustive research, would have written. But it is a balanced view of the Founder's life and presents William Marsh Rice as a warm human being, the center of a drama of no mean proportions. I am confident that Professor Muir would be pleased.

Katherine Fischer Drew
Editor
Rice University Studies

PREFACE

Ever since I was a graduate student in the Institute in 1940 I have been interested in William Marsh Rice. I was astonished then, and I remain astonished, that so little information was available on the founder and so little interest in him evinced by members of the university community. . . .The two questions which fascinate me are What sort of man was Rice? and How did he accumulate his fortune?

—A. F. Muir

This was the task to which Andrew Forest Muir addressed himself and for which he was granted a Guggenheim Fellowship in 1957, but the work remained incomplete at the time of his death in 1969. The extent and variety of the notes and manuscripts left by Dr. Muir, nevertheless, are ample evidence of the range of his research and the zest which he brought to its pursuit. I feel greatly privileged to have had access to this material.

Nothing, however, is more certain than that it is well-nigh impossible for one person to take over another's research material and from this turn out anything like the study which the original writer intended. In the case of Andrew Forest Muir, who possessed a singularly felicitous turn of phrase, a wide and exhaustive acquaintance with Texas history, and a feeling for the fine shades of human behavior by which everything became grist to his mill, such an undertaking is especially difficult. I have done my best to retain the scope and depth of Dr. Muir's work; undoubtedly mistakes have crept in—for these I alone am responsible.

A number of people have gone out of their way to be of assistance to this project, and those to whom particular thanks are due include Barbara Hamilton and Ola Moore, archivists at the Fondren Library; Peter Rippe, of the Harris County Heritage Society; Ben Blanton and Nathan Broch of the Rice University Office of Information Services; Willoughby Williams and Sam Emison of Development; John F. O'Neil of the Department of Fine Arts; and the history secretaries, Linda Barnes and Linda Quaidy, for their masterful interpretation of a bewildering manuscript. I should like to add that without the patience and encouragement of Katherine Fischer Drew, Chairman of the Department of History, the entire project might have died a-borning, and to thank Mrs. Richard W. Neff, Sr., for her generosity with her time and interest and for pointing out that Patty Hall Rice's Christian name, like that of Thomas Jefferson's favorite daughter, was most probably Martha.

Sylvia S. Morris

May, 1972

RICE UNIVERSITY STUDIES

Vol. 58, No. 2   Spring 1972

WILLIAM MARSH RICE AND HIS INSTITUTE
A BIOGRAPHICAL STUDY

WILLIAM MARSH RICE IN HIS LATER YEARS

CHAPTER I

THE EARLY YEARS

"Just below Springfield," wrote the Reverend Timothy Dwight, that indefatigable traveler and preacher who was soon to become the president of Yale University, as he journeyed northward along the Connecticut River valley at the end of the eighteenth century, "we crossed a vigorous millstream on which, a little eastward, is erected the most considerable manufactory of arms in the United States."[1]

By 1812, when David Rice, the third to bear that name, moved his young family to Springfield from Norfolk County, Massachusetts, and went to work in the forging-shop at the Springfield Armory,[2] the town had changed very little. For "a few hundred dollars," David Rice bought a square clapboard house of one and one-half stories on Hickory Street,[3] perhaps not anticipating that four-month-old Louisa was to be the first of ten children. A son, David, was born two years later, and a second, William, in March 1816; Josiah and Lucy Ann, who followed in 1819 and 1821, respectively, both died in infancy; but Minerva, Caleb, Charlotte, and Frederick, who followed at intervals of about two years, lived and thrived. The last of David Rice's daughters, Susan, did not long survive her birth in 1833.[4]

The Hickory Street house stood at no great distance from the Armory's Middle Watershops; with an accessible and abundant supply of waterpower, these continued to expand and David Rice advanced from working in the forging-shop to the boring of gun barrels and the making of bayonets, until in 1833 he was appointed an Inspector of the Watershops.[5] It was a position of some importance, which brought with it added responsibilities, and undoubtedly neither David Rice nor Patty, his wife, had the

1

time to single out any one of their children for particular notice; certainly, there is very little known about their second son, William Marsh Rice, during this Springfield period of his life.

Central Massachusetts must nonetheless have been a pleasant place to grow up. Timothy Dwight observed that Springfield was the oldest town in Hampshire County (from which, in David Rice's day, Hampden County had been separated), lying along a single street on the western side of the Connecticut River. "An uncommon appearance of neatness prevails almost everywhere, refreshing the eye of the traveller."[6] By 1816, the year of William Marsh Rice's birth, the established pattern of New England existence, manufacture and trade, had been firmly laid down; merchandise went inland all over upper New England and, via a line of stages and transport wagons, as far to the west as Albany. The Springfield Armory, whose only Federal counterpart was at Harper's Ferry on the Potomac River, was turning out ten thousand muskets annually as well as bayonets, fieldpieces, mortars, and howitzers.[7] Prosperity was on the rise: the next few years were to see the establishment in Springfield of a paper mill, a brewery, and factories which turned out cutlery and cotton goods,[8] while by 1828 Thomas Blanchard's stern-wheeler, the *Blanchard,* had already made the trip downstream to Hartford in an astonishing two hours and twenty minutes.[9]

The Reverend Mr. Dwight, always prompt to round off his journal entries with an edifying moral, found one ready-made in the Connecticut Valley. Its inhabitants, he remarked, "are so remote from a market as to be perfectly free from that sense of inferiority customarily felt by the body of people who live in the neighborhood of large cities. Hence a superior spirit of personal independence is generated and cherished."[10] "There is no tract of land of the same size in which learning is more, or more uniformly, encouraged,"[11] he added, and that observation is borne out by the character of men like David Rice.

Only once, so far as is presently known, did William Marsh Rice speak directly about his parents, in a letter written to one of his sisters (most probably Charlotte) in the spring of 1899.

Reflecting that he and she were no longer young, he looked back toward the past: "Our childhood had many pleasent hours . . . and the troubles were soon forgotten. Fathers and Mothers thoughts were mostly devoted to their chrilden. I do not think they worried very much. Father had so *firm* a reliance upon providence that nothing seemed to lay heavy on his mind—though he was sensative which could be seen at times."[12] (Rice's spelling was always distinctly his own.) Providence, however, could not be made responsible for that which man could effect; as a freeholder of Hampden County David Rice served at various times both as tax assessor and tax collector for the town of Springfield and "climaxed his political career in 1827 by representing the town in the General Court of Massachusetts."[13] When he left his position at the Armory in 1843, after its administration had undergone a substantial change, and moved his family to South Belchertown, Massachusetts, he was again elected tax assessor and subsequently justice of the peace.[14]

This much public service was expected of almost any New England property owner; where David Rice went further than most was in his lifelong efforts on behalf of his church and the cause of education. Although Methodist preachers had occasionally come through Springfield as early as 1796, holding meetings in private homes wherever those were made available, the first regular Society was organized in 1815 at the Upper Watershops by the Reverend William Marsh, of the Tolland, Connecticut, circuit.[15] The first two members to be admitted were David and Patty Rice and the son who was born to them the following spring, although he was not christened until June 1820, was named for William Marsh, the pioneering circuit rider.[16]

In that same year, 1820, the Methodist Episcopal Society got together three hundred dollars with which to put up a "house for publick worship,"[17] having up till then still met wherever occasion offered, including such places as the courthouse and David Rice's barn.[18] The *Centennial Souvenir of the New England Conference* records that "David Rice offered to give the land, a building committee was appointed and materials were upon the ground before the people knew what was going on. Monday the frame was put up, and the following Sunday services were held in Asbury Chapel."[19] David Rice, never a man to rest on his laurels, went on to serve at different times as parish steward, trustee, moderator, overseer of the poor, member of the parish committee, and superintendant of funerals for this growing congregation.[20]

Timothy Dwight's observations on the encouragement of learning in the Connecticut Valley were not altogether accurate for the town of Springfield. Until 1825, the common district schools of that place were conducted, according to a history of Hampden County published at the turn of the century, "with reference to economy rather than the welfare of the youth."[21] An article which ran in the Houston *Chronicle* in 1916, on the one hundredth anniversary of William Marsh Rice's birth, described in rather arch detail the "one-story school" (probably a one-room schoolhouse) where the smallest children were sent more to get them out from underfoot than for the sake of educating them; one Springfield worthy who claimed to have been a schoolmate of Rice's recounted that the teacher used to sweep a spot clean on the schoolhouse floor so that the littlest ones could curl up there and go to sleep.[22]

In 1826, however, most likely through the efforts of men like David Rice, an act was passed which required every town in Massachusetts of five hundred families or more to provide for the benefit of its children a schoolmaster who could give instruction in United States history, bookkeeping, geometry, surveying, and algebra.[23] Springfield had by then extended itself along both banks of the river and numbered something over a thousand householders; in the following April a committee of seven, including David Rice, was formed to see to the construction of a new school and the town voted $500 toward this purpose.[24] On the first of September, 1828,[25] the Classical High School with its cupola, bell and "proper outhouse" stood ready to receive the first classes composed of fifty-three boys with an average age of twelve years.[26] At the first annual examination in August, 1829, the fifty boys taking part showed "special proficiency" in algebra, natural philosophy, and mental arithmetic.[27]

William Marsh Rice was exactly twelve years old in that opening autumn; it seems safe to assume that he would have been one of the first to be enrolled. Yet four years later, in the spring of 1832, his name was not included on the roster of students;[28] this may have been merely due to error, but most of the anecdotes told about his early life agree that he left school at around the age of fifteen to go to work as a clerk in the Family Grocery Store owned and operated on the ground floor of the town hall on State Street by a retired whaling captain named Henry L. Bunker.[29] Perhaps after three years young William felt he had absorbed all the surveying, geometry, and natural philosophy he was likely to need; perhaps the presence of so many children in the small house on Hickory Street meant that Patty Rice found it hard to make ends meet. Or schoolboy games and recitations may simply not have held as much interest for William Marsh Rice as the intricacies of making money. If indeed he did drop out, it cannot have given his father much satisfaction, for David Rice's commitment to education was as firm as ever: the Wesleyan Academy, newly transplanted to Wilbraham, Massachusetts, from South Newmarket, New Hampshire, listed him among its earliest trustees[30] and it is on record that both Charlotte and Frederick Rice, William's favorite sister and brother, went on in later years to graduate there.[31]

David Rice lived to be seventy-seven, dying in 1867 on the farm at Three Rivers, Massachusetts, where he had moved from South Belchertown in the last year of his life.[32] A photograph apparently made in his late sixties shows a handsome man with thick white hair, high cheekbones, and a determined set to his jaw: the face of a Highland crofter or an old Indian fighter. In his will he left five dollars to each of his surviving sons, "if demanded within one year from my decease," instructions for the payment of his just debts, and the remainder of his estate, subsequently valued at $1365, was left to his "faithful and beloved Wife Patty." Along with a horse, a cow, furniture, stoves and bed clothes, Patty Rice inherited one "string of old sleigh-bells."[33]

Of Patty Hall Rice there is almost nothing on record. William Marsh Rice, in that same letter quoted above in which he spoke of his father's reliance on Providence, goes on to say that his parents "both worked so hard. It was a great comfort to me that I was able to relieve them towards the end."[34] Rice's sisters, Charlotte and Minerva, spoke in their old age of the continual stream of gifts for his parents and sisters which found its way to Massachusetts after the end of the War Between the States. "When he was visiting father he left $100 with me for him"[35] was a fairly common statement in their correspondence. With a good deal of care, William Marsh Rice chose a set of cameos for Minerva, "trinkets" and jewelry for his nieces, and "sixty or seventy yards of silk" to be made into dresses for his mother and Charlotte.[36] The house at Three Rivers in which his father and mother spent the last years of their lives, Patty Rice living on there until 1877, was his gift. In the year after its purchase he sent up carpets and parlor furniture from New York to accommodate the household which by then included Charlotte Mc-Kee and her husband and children.[37]

Charlotte Rice McKee, giving testimony in the long litigation suit that followed the death of William Marsh Rice's second wife, made one brief but telling observation which reflected on the character of both her mother and her late sister-in-law. Her brother William, she made clear, had never brought his new bride up to Massachusetts after their marriage to meet his relatives; Patty Hall Rice, a "spunky old lady," had taken against the newcomer sight unseen, and William felt that his wife's presence at Three Rivers would mean nothing but trouble.[38] Patty Rice's spunkiness is not to be wondered at, considering the history of her father, the old Revolutionary War soldier Josiah Hall, who in so many ways seemed to have served as the model for his grandson William.

Josiah Hall was born in South Walpole, Massachusetts, on December 26, 1753, and died in the same township on July 15, 1855, at the not inconsiderable age of 101 years, 6 months, and

20 days.[39] His photograph, preserved in the archives of Rice University with his name and dates recorded on the back in what appears to be his grandson's handwriting, is as clear as if it had just been taken. Evidently well into his eighties, in an admirably cut broadcloth coat, high collar, and what looks like a black satin cravat, the old soldier folds his hands on the head of his cane and gazes squarely into the camera. His hair, as thick as his son-in-law's, curls crisply over his ears and the source of those "expressive" blue eyes which in William Marsh Rice "seemed to pierce through a stranger at a glance"[40] is easily apparent.

The affinity between William Marsh Rice and his maternal grandfather went deeper than appearances. In April, 1775, Josiah Hall had responded to the alarm at Lexington by marching off to join Captain Seth Bullard's company near Roxbury, Massachusetts.[41] Reenlisting twice before the war's end, he campaigned as far south as New Jersey, took part in the battle of Port Chester, and was there struck by a musket ball on the "ancle."[42] Off and on during the last thirty-five years of his life, Josiah was engaged in a brisk running engagement with the United States War Department over the matter of his pension. Granted in 1818 in an order signed by John C. Calhoun, it was revoked in 1820 on the grounds that Hall was the owner of considerable property.[43] Undaunted, he submitted a fresh claim under a new Act of Congress of 1832 and succeeded in having the pension reinstated. By November, 1845, it had occurred to him that his original ten days' service after the call to arms at Lexington had never been allowed for and that this entitled him to an additional $1.10 a month. William Ellis, certifying in 1845 as to the authenticity of claim and claimant in Ellis' capacity as justice of the peace for the county of Norfolk, Massachusetts, could not refrain from adding a comment of his own. "I would just say that said Hall tho aged appears to have a very clear and correct memory about Revolutionary transactions."[44] The War Department evidently felt the same way, for the requested increase was granted without further delay, which did not prevent Josiah, some three months before his death, from initiating a whole new action to obtain bounty lands under yet another Act recently passed by Congress. It is hard not to assume that he would have been successful.

In all likelihood, William Marsh Rice did not see his grandfather's exchanges with the War Department and so was spared a phrase that appears as part of the claim of 1820 which could only have pained him. "I am indebted to sundry persons," declared Josiah without ceremony, "in the sum of $629."[45] From his first days with Captain Bunker, being in debt was something which Josiah's grandson scrupulously avoided. After between four and five years on State Street, filling customers' orders for the wheat and flour which the Captain habitually kept on hand and the fresh fruit which he offered as a delicacy at Thanksgiving,[46] young Rice struck out on his own. With David Rice to cosign his note, since he himself had not yet attained his majority, William Rice bought out another store closer to the Watershops and in less than two years had cleared two thousand dollars in this first business venture.[47]

The earliest financial statement which exists concerning this man who went on to become a millionaire several times over, and the only one associated with Springfield, is in the Springfield city clerk's offices among the mortgages of personal property. Against the sum of forty dollars tendered him by William M. Rice in December 1837, one William W. Bowles pledged to said Rice various articles of personal property, including "1 live geese feather bed," one "French Bedsteadd," one mahogany table and one made of cherrywood, six chairs, one stove, and "one gilt looking glass," should Bowles fail to repay the loan at the end of a year.[48] No doubt Charlotte, Louisa, and Minerva would have enjoyed admiring themselves in the gilt mirror and Patty Rice could only have been glad of a feather-bed in the Massachusetts winters, but there is no record of whether William Marsh Rice ever took possession of these items. By the following December, when the loan fell due, Rice had gone like so many others to seek his fortune in Texas.

Captain James A. Baker, Jr., a close personal and business associate of Rice during his later years, in an address delivered in 1931 at the sixteenth Commencement Convocation of the

Rice Institute, did not hesitate to attribute the founder's removal to Texas to romantic motives. "His young and ardent soul was fired with the spirit of patriotism and adventure, and he then and there resolved to emigrate to Texas and cast his fortune with those heroic souls who at San Jacinto had humbled the Napoleon of the West."[49] With all due respect for Captain Baker, it seems more likely that Rice left Springfield for hardheaded practical reasons. Santa Anna's defeat and the emergence of a new republic in the Southwest had been widely reported throughout the East, and men whom Rice may have known, like the Springfield tailor, Elam Stockbridge, had already moved on to try their luck on the frontier,[50] drawn by the rumors of wealth beyond the Sabine River. In 1837 the Springfield newspapers took the view that the proposed admission of Texas to the United States would be an economic disaster for the rest of the country[51] and poked fun at the frontiersmen as well by solemnly asserting that currency under the Lone Star consisted of "cows for large sums" with calves thrown in for change.[52]

More directly to the point, by the late summer of 1837 the United States had entered a period of financial panic, partly as a result of unwise land speculation, partly due to President Andrew Jackson's "hard money" policies, which produced several years of depression. Business in Springfield, like business everywhere, can only have fallen off sharply. William Marsh Rice, along with many others, could have seen a notice carried by Eastern newspapers the previous summer: the brothers Augustus C. and John K. Allen, having availed themselves of a sizable chunk of Gulf Coast land, did not intend for the opportunity thereby provided to go unremarked. In an outburst of salesmanship and self-confidence that indicated better than they knew the shape of things to come, the Allens submitted some first-rate promotional material to the press of New Orleans, Mobile, Louisville, Washington, and New York.

THE TOWN OF HOUSTON
Situated at the head of navigation on the west bank of Buffalo river

is now for the first time brought to public notice, because, until now, the properties were not ready to offer to the public, with the advantages of capital and improvements.

The town of Houston is located at a point on the river which must ever command the trade of the largest and richest portion of Texas . . . .There is no place in Texas more healthy, having an abundance of excellent spring water and enjoying the sea breeze in all its freshness.

No place in Texas possesses so many advantages for building, having fine ash, cedar and oak in inexhaustible quantities, also the tall and beautiful magnolia grows in abundance. In the vicinity are fine quarries of stone.

Nature appears to have designated this place for the future seat of government. It is handsome and beautifully elevated, salubrious and well watered and now in the very heart or center of population, and will be so for a length of time to come.[53]

From the very first John Allen had intended for his new city to become the capital of the Republic of Texas and on December 15, 1836, it was so designated by the congress, to continue as such until 1840.[54] Although on January 1, 1837, the town still consisted of tents, with the sole exception of the Allens' log house, building went ahead so rapidly that congress could meet there on schedule May 1, in a Capitol that still lacked a roof.[55] Looking at a map of the southwestern United States, William Marsh Rice would have recognized a situation with an unlimited potential for business growth when he saw one. In cannily buying up their land at the highest navigable point on the "Buffalo river," the Allen brothers established Houston as the furthest point inland on the wide crescent between the Sabine and the Rio Grande where goods could be shipped directly by water. The westward push of settlers could only continue and the Texas legislature was doing its bit by promising 1280 acres of free land to any family man moving into the Republic between March, 1836 and October, 1837. This grant was later reduced to 640 acres, but that figure still represented more than any man could farm on his own and for many years the grantee was neither obliged to live on, nor to improve, his holdings.[56]

An opening frontier stands in need of any and every sort of

finished goods; tradition, once again the only apparent source of information, says that William Marsh Rice sent a shipment of merchandise around to Galveston by sea while making the journey there himself down the Ohio and Mississippi by rail and packet.[57] The "shanties and stumps about the street"[58] which greeted him in October, 1838, cannot have looked any better when he was given the news that all his goods had been lost at sea along with the ship carrying them. Whether because of this setback or in spite of it, Rice chose not to remain in Galveston, for on February 12, 1839, he was issued a conditional headright certificate to 320 acres of land by the Harrisburg County board of commissioners in the town of Houston.[59]

Unless some Massachusetts attic yields up unexpected treasure and discloses whatever letters Rice sent home during his first months in Texas, life in that city where he spent the next twenty-five years can only be observed through the eyes of other contemporary visitors. Telling of her journey up the bayou to the spot where John Allen had hacked away the coffee weeds with his bowie knife only a few years before to lay out a landing, a young Englishwoman became rhapsodic over the enormous magnolias, laurels, bay, arbutus, and rhododendrons which met overhead as the steamer "wound through the short reaches of this most lovely stream."[60] She evidently had the advantage of fine weather, for William Fairfax Gray's wife, making the same trip in January, found the bayou alarmingly full of snags and the "tenacious black clay" in the town itself a sore trial to her housewifely pride.[61] All the same, in 1839 Milly Gray found a one and a half-story house, built of concrete mixed with oyster shell, waiting for her instead of a tent;[62] the Jockey Club had just announced its spring meeting; and the Reverend Richard Salmon, an Episcopal priest from New York, had advertised the opening of a Primary School that stressed "the higher branches of science" in the previous November.[63] Two theaters were already flourishing and the year before a travelling company had come out from New Orleans to put on "The School For Scandal."[64]

To be sure, there were some drawbacks to the Allens' earthly

paradise. In the absence of any sawmill in the immediate vicinity, lumber was hard to come by and sometimes had to be
shipped from as far away as Maine[65] (the Grays brought theirs
with them from Virginia and then had indescribable difficulties
getting it hauled from Galveston to Houston); merchants in
New Orleans, feeling the pinch of hard times, began to refuse
credit to their Texas clients, and Houston was visited by its first
disastrous epidemic of yellow fever, which raged on until a
norther on the twentieth of November dropped the temperature
to forty degrees Fahrenheit.[66]

Having neither womenfolk to make comfortable nor children
to educate, William Marsh Rice seems to have settled down at
once to the business of making money, for on April 22, 1839,
an agreement was recorded between W. M. Rice and Reed and
Eichelberger whereby the said W. M. Rice "doth agree to furnish with Liquors the Bar of the Milam House, occupied by the
above named Reed & Eichelberger," for which he was to receive, over and above the cost of the liquors, three dollars per
day and board.[67] James Baker, speaking in 1931 with the instinc-
tive discretion of the barrister, preferred to omit this episode
from his account of the founder's history, thereby sacrificing
one of the authentic colorful incidents in the career of a man
who throughout his life neither smoked nor drank anything
even as stimulating as coffee or tea.[68]

The wine and spirits business, in any event, could not have
offered more than a limited future, and Rice must have already
formed a fairly shrewd idea of where his real opportunities lay.
Less than two months later, on the first of June, he and one
Timothy Kingsbury bought of Horace Eggleston three and one-
half lots in San Felipe, Austin County, executing notes to Eggleston for something over half the purchase price.[69] Rice had
resold the same lots by November, having apparently bought
out Kingsbury's share in the meantime, and he had also moved
on into another rewarding area of Texas commercial life: he was
prepared to furnish cash against mortgages on property.[70]

The Texas constitutional convention of 1835 had "denounced
and prohibited banks" within the Republic. As a result, until the

adoption of the state constitution of 1870 there were to be no banks chartered in Texas[71]—which was apparently "the way the farmer-planter-dominated legislature preferred it"—in the hope of discouraging industry.[72] Banking services had perforce to be carried on in a number of rather loosely defined ways: successful mercantile firms extended credit as part of their business transactions, thereby playing the part of private banks, and promissory notes were traded like cash.

> Depreciated banknotes from the United States circulated widely; . . . some of this paper was issued by wildcat, or even nonexistent, banks in other states. Passers and accepters had sometimes to guess its worth . . . . When hard money was essential, the major medium of exchange was old Spanish or Mexican pesos or dollars and their fractions . . . . It was customary to smash the image of the King of Spain on the older coins with a hammer, or to deface the Mexican eagle. Such mutilation in no way damaged bullion value and did assuage national pride.[73]

By the summer of 1840 Rice had entered into the first of his several business partnerships, for on August 5 "William M. Rice and Barnabas Haskill, merchants residing and trading in the city of Houston," leased the Austin House property on Block 21 from Benjamin P. Buckner for the sum of $50 monthly.[74] The partnership must have been short-lived, for in August of the following year the lease was renewed in Rice's name alone.[75] Posterity can only speculate about Haskill (or Haskoll or Haskell as it was variously spelled), since no records touching on his career in Houston have been found besides the fact of his arrival from Connecticut, his membership in the First Baptist Church, and his apparent departure from Texas in the winter of 1841-42.[76]

It may have been that Mrs. Haskill found the Southwest, after Connecticut, too alarming for her taste, for in the spring of 1842 Santa Anna, in a show of force to keep up the claim of Mexican sovereignty over Texas, was to send an expedition north across the Rio Grande that easily captured San Antonio. Sam Houston hastily moved the government from Austin down to the city that bore his name but the Mexicans rode south again after only a few days. Although the Texas militia had rushed to the colors and a company from Houston actually set out on a mission of rescue, the President prudently vetoed his Congress' declaration of war and the men had marched only sixty miles when an order was issued for their return.[77] Under the command of Captain Sidney Sherman was a private named William Marsh Rice;[78] it was to be his first and last experience of military service. The Mexicans repeated their feint in September and this time Houston was forced to order a pursuit as far south as Laredo, but Rice took no part in it. Unlike his grandfather Josiah, he must not have found soldiering to his taste.

Military glory, on the other hand, seems to have appealed to the man who by December, 1844, had become Rice's partner in an association that was to last for a good many years and lay the solid foundations of the Rice fortune. Ebenezer B. Nichols was likewise a Yankee who in 1833 with a load of lumber had come out to Texas from Cooperstown, New York. For a time he campaigned enthusiastically against both Indians and Mexicans, eventually rising to the rank of major.[79] Many years later, following a flood on the Colorado River at Austin in April, 1900, William Marsh Rice enquired of another old friend if it had not been at just about that spot "that Capt or Col Pierce & Lieut Nichols and orderly Marks fought the Indians in 1839? Can you remember that far back and are you and I the only persons left from so long ago?"[80] In the end, Nichols settled down in Houston, where he soon turned "a handsome profit" exporting pecans to New Orleans out of Port Lavaca.[81]

The firm of Rice and Nichols had its offices on Main Street in Houston and proceeded to carry on, on a far more ambitious scale, the kind of business that William Marsh Rice had first practiced back in Springfield. As commission and forwarding merchants, Rice and Nichols brought in goods from New Orleans and from as far away as New York, first by boat up the Buffalo Bayou from Galveston and then by ox wagon to the settlers and plantation owners further inland. History is often best recorded on shopping lists, and a good deal can be deduced about life in Texas in the eighteen-thirties and -forties from the ledgers of Rice and Nichols. Already in September, 1844, William Marsh Rice was assuring the Secretary of the Treasury in Austin that he would send to New Orleans "at the first opportunity" for the articles which had been requested, to wit, paperweights, quills, sealing-wax, sand, red ink, inkstands, and that bureaucratic essential, red tape; by the twenty-fifth of October these had been sent forward to Austin "in great haste."[82] On Christmas Eve the *Morning Star* advertised that Rice and Nichols had "now received a full supply of groceries"[83] and a few years later the Rice firm's account with Mrs. E. G. Compton makes it clear that the ladies of the Gulf Coast did not intend to be outstripped by their Eastern sisters when it came to questions of fashion. An occasional keg of nails, or gallon of brandy, reflects the presence of the male members of the Compton household, but the accounts run heavily to Swiss muslin, Irish linen, whalebone, white satin ribbons, black silk, cambric, hooks and eyes, and—presumably for the servants—"callico" and "2 doz palm hats."[84]

While there seemed to be no end to the variety of goods that flowed into Texas, her principal export increasingly came to be cotton. Whereas in 1839 only eight bales had been sent down to the coast from Houston, by 1841 Cornelius Ennis, one of William Marsh Rice's lifelong friends, had made the first shipment of cotton direct to Boston from the port of Galveston.[85] William M. Rice and other prominent merchants of the city, in that same year, offered a prize of a gold cup to the planter who brought in the first twenty bales; a silver one for the first five.[86] In the spring of 1844 the first cotton compress was brought to Houston and the following year it was estimated that the number of bales to be shipped out of the city would run to nearly fifteen thousand.[87] Hides ran a poor second to cotton, as did lumber after a sawmill had been set up alongside the bayou in the middle eighteen-forties.[88] It may be noted that about the same time "Mr. Elim Stockbridge," having apparently discovered that there did not seem to be a great demand for gentlemen's frock coats on the prairie, put up Houston's first cornmill, which stood on the north side of the bayou and was powered by three oxen walking a treadmill.[89]

"Persons Controlling or owning Cotton should be prepared to take Care of it and let it lay. The lower it drops the greater the advance. I have been familiar [with] and handled More or less Cotton for More than fifty years," William Marsh Rice wrote briskly to one of his Texas agents some four months before his death.[90] Always seeing a little farther ahead in the business world than the next man, Rice was quick to realize that a cotton economy was inevitably dependent upon the availability of transportation: every bale that came into the city of Houston, whether from the rich Brazos bottom lands or from as far north as Dallas and Waco, had been dragged there by ox teams, eight to twelve pair to a hitch.[91] By late autumn and early winter, when the bulk of the planters' crop was ready to market, the roads could become impassable for weeks at a time; that "tenacious black clay" which had been such a trial in Milly Gray's parlor was an even greater disaster for teams and wagons.

Rice was not alone in wishing that something could be done about the transportation situation. Early in 1850, the builder of the world's first plank road, running from Brewerton, New York, to Syracuse, a Yankee named Harvey Baldwin, came to Houston on a visit to his sister, Charlotte, who had married Augustus Allen before he and his brother John set out for the Southwest. Baldwin publicized his project so successfully that although preliminary grading had been undertaken a full ten years earlier for a railroad that would connect Harrisburg, just down the bayou from Houston, with the Brazos Valley,[92] a public meeting was held in Houston on April eighteenth to debate the question of plank roads. William Marsh Rice was appointed at that meeting to a committee whose business it was to study the proposal and to outline the incorporation of the Houston and Brazos Plank Road Company.[93]

The committee quickly came to the agreement that plank roads were a sound investment and surveying got under way almost at once. Rice, however, who liked to keep all his options open, was in that same year one of the incorporators of the

Buffalo Bayou, Brazos and Colorado Railway, a company backed by a group of Boston entrepreneurs who had taken over the ownership of the townsite of Harrisburg and hoped, by transforming it into a rail center, to overtake the Allens' upstart settlement higher up the bayou. Rice and the other Houstonians who invested in the company were undoubtedly less interested in the future of Harrisburg than in the benefits which rail transport might bring to themselves; by 1852, when the Buffalo Bayou, Brazos and Colorado had actually begun to lay track out toward the Brazos bottoms,[94] plank roads were heard of no more.

The honor of being the first railroad incorporated in Texas, however, had already gone to the Galveston and Red River Railway in 1848, the brainchild of one of those colorful and gifted men who so often seemed drawn to the republic in the early years of its history. Paul Bremond was the son of a French doctor, Paul Barlie Bremond, who had emigrated to the United States in 1805 and married an American girl from Fishkill, New York.[95] Their son, Paul, was born in October, 1810, and left school at the age of twleve to go to work as a hatter's apprentice; unsuccessful when he tried to set up in business for himself, he moved to Philadelphia in 1830 and tried again, this time with better luck for he is reported to have made some $40,000 by the end of six years.[96] Like so many others, he saw himself ruined by the same panic of 1837 which had driven William Marsh Rice out of Springfield, and Paul Bremond resolved to move to Galveston, at that time the largest city in Texas with a population of some three thousand. Unlike Rice, he took with him a wife and two small children, but he also was faced with the loss of his furniture as well as of the merchandise he had sent around from Philadelphia when the brig carrying them was lost within sight of Galveston Island.[97]

Helped out by friends, Bremond first set up a small store and later an auction and commission business. Around 1842 he moved himself and his family to Houston and prospered in much the same manner that William Marsh Rice had done. His attention turned more and more, however, to the problems of transportation in general and of railroads in particular; the latter never ceased to fascinate him. A believer in spiritualism and the founder of a small society for its study in Houston, he claimed that spirit advisors were responsible for his railroad projects, urging him on whenever he allowed his efforts to flag.[98] "Seemingly he was being advised by the best railroad talent in purgatory, for not only did he actually build a railroad, but indeed he built on a shoestring one of the most valuable railroad properties in the United States."[99]

Paul Bremond threw up the first shovelful of dirt for the Houston and Texas Central Railway, as the Galveston and Red River was shortly rechristened, on January 1, 1853.[100] Always short of funds, he seems often to have gotten track laid on the strength of his persuasiveness alone, but his debts were all settled with scrupulous honesty once the road began to pay off. After his first wife's death in 1846, leaving him with three children, he had married Mary Van Alstyne, the daughter of one of his business partners, who bore him five daughters; six years after her death in 1864 he married the American-born Vicomtesse de Valernes.[101] In a photograph taken in 1875, he could easily have passed for a cultivated Frenchman of the Second Empire; his jackets were cut, all his life, after the fashions of Philadelphia and New York and he affected a stock in the place of a necktie. Only the red ribbon of the Legion of Honor is missing.

The early days of the Houston and Texas Central were invariably lively.

> It was pushed out of Houston somewhat north of west toward the Brazos River, and since within a few miles of town it began to cross a waterlogged and often impassable prairie, it became profitable even before it reached the point where it turned northward. At this point some of the officers and stockholders of the company laid out the town of Hempstead. Because of the great number of accidents that the H & T C had, it was affectionately referred to as the Angel Maker, and because of the propensity that the residents of Hempstead had for shooting at one another, the place was known as Sixshooter Junction. There were times, as trains passed through Hempstead, that passengers found it advisable to get out of their seats and lie on the floor.[102]

In that same year of plank roads and railways, 1850, William Marsh Rice was thirty-four. He had been living in Houston for eleven years and occupied a recognized position as one of the city's most substantial men; from now on, nearly everything he touched would turn to gold. The portrait which was made about this time and now hangs in the entrance hall of the restored Nichols-Rice-Cherry house, shows a man in the prime of life, shrewd and somewhat quizzical. Time and varnish have darkened the artist's original colors; those "clear, expressive blue eyes" described by Frank McKee some fifty years afterward could be taken for hazel; the hair is still thick and very dark. There is little evidence of the "frank open countenance" remembered by McKee; here is the face of a man who believed in keeping his own counsel. Increasingly preoccupied as he was with his own health in later years, Rice appears nonetheless to have been a wiry man, rather small in stature, who was rarely ill. At the time of his death he was reported to measure only five feet three inches in height and to weigh ninety pounds,[103] but age had undoubtedly diminished both weight and stature. There is nothing frail about the man in the Rice House portrait.

With the arrival of prosperity, William Marsh Rice had begun to send for other members of his family, since Massachusetts still did not seem to hold much in the way of opportunity. First to arrive was his elder brother, David, who was far and away the most dashing member of the family: "one of the handsomest men to be found anywhere" with a complexion like a girl's.[104] Married in Springfield at the age of twenty, he was a young widower by the time he came out to Texas leaving two sons in Massachusetts with David and Patty Rice.[105] Striking out from Galveston, he apparently worked for a while for his brother and then moved on into the Texas Rangers, where he rose to the rank of colonel.[106] He is mentioned as the treasurer of Houston's Hook and Ladder Company No. 1 in 1861,[107] but nowhere else, so far as is known, in the city's records; possibly he did not share the singleminded devotion to business that characterized most of his relatives. The coming of the Civil War gave him what he had been looking for in the shape of a commission in Hood's Texas Brigade.

Rice's brothers Caleb and Frederick made their way to Texas at about the same time, which is reported to have been 1850, although Caleb, nine years younger than William, returned to New England after only a short stay and remained there until his death in 1865.[108] Frederick, who had been born in 1830, seems to have been William all over again. The last-born of David and Patty Hall Rice's children to survive infancy, he was very close to his elder brother, who had seen to it that Frederick as well as Charlotte stayed on to graduate from the Wilbraham Academy.[109] Charlotte, writing to William in the autumn of 1898, gives us one rare glimpse back into their childhood. "How rapidly time flies," wrote the old lady. "It seems but a short time since Fred and I were children at home and I remember how we used to run down to your store."[110]

When Frederick Rice arrived in Houston, he had already been working for a year as a clerk in the firm of McGilvary and Company in Palmer, Massachusetts, and went straight into his elder brother's business.[111] The two men seem to have remained close all their lives and William Marsh Rice, who was to remain childless in spite of his two marriages, took more than an uncle's ordinary interest in the welfare of Frederick's children. A burgeoning frontier town like Houston is not only a likely place for younger brothers to seek their fortunes; it is also notoriously favorable to young women who are looking for husbands. When Frederick Rice was married in August, 1854, in Syracuse, New York, to Charlotte Baldwin Randon, it can only be presumed that he had met the striking young widow in Texas at the home of her father, Horace Baldwin, or of her aunt, Mrs. Augustus C. Allen, who was also named Charlotte. The Baldwins tended to migrate from New York to Houston somewhat en bloc: Horace, brother not only to Charlotte Allen but also to that Harvey Baldwin who had initiated the Plank Road venture, had come out about 1839 and within five years was elected mayor of Houston.[112] Besides Charlotte Randon Rice he had a younger daughter, Julia Elizabeth, who had also married and for the time being played no part in Rice family history.

William Marsh Rice seems to have set his younger brother an example in all things, not excluding matrimony. On June 29, 1850, in Christ Church, where since 1845 he had been a member of the vestry, he had been married to Margaret Bremond, Paul Bremond's eighteen-year-old daughter.[113] On the evening of the wedding there was a reception at the Capitol Hotel described as "the most splendid affair ever given in the city" and the following day the Rices set off on a wedding trip to the Atlantic seaboard.[114] Travel was notoriously unhurried in those days; the honeymooners may have only been returning home when in the following February William Marsh Rice telegraphed ahead to Louisville from somewhere in Ohio or Kentucky asking that the steamer *Oregon* be held for them a few hours. The *Oregon* could not wait and set off without the Rices; on the second of March she exploded and sank near Island Number 22 in the Mississippi.[115]

In the archives of the Fondren Library at Rice University there is a portrait said to be of Margaret Bremond Rice. Artist and date are unknown; it does not appear to have been done as a companion piece to the one of her husband referred to earlier and, although in his last years William Marsh Rice expressed an interest in having himself photographed,[116] he never refers to the existence of either of these paintings. Margaret Rice's face is a haunting one, not pretty in any conventional sense but intelligent and with more than a trace of humor. She is dressed with elegant simplicity in a lace-edged *robe de style* of bronzed green velvet, a Paisley shawl in dark orange thrown across her right arm. Her only jewels are a cameo showing a classic dwelling or temple, with earrings that match. Her eyes and her hair, which is worn in the style made fashionable by the Empress Eugenie, are both dark, and there are faint lines of fatigue, or perhaps of illness, around her mouth. It is a face full of repose, perfectly complementing her husband's.

One of Rice's characteristics was a strong sense of the proper order of things; having acquired a charming young wife, he next required a residence that would serve not only to show her off but also to reflect the solid state of his fortune, valued at that time at $25,000.[117] He did not have far to look, for he and

Ebenezer Nichols had recently decided that in the interests of their business one of the partners should move to Galveston, through which all the firm's goods sooner or later passed. Nichols elected to make the change, believing that the future was brighter down on the coast; the new home which he had just begun to build for himself he sold to his obliging partner.

According to tradition, although almost certainly incorrectly, Nichols' building materials had been intended for the construction of a warship and were sold to him by mistake. The heart-pine sills, running the length of the house, measured 18 by 24 inches and were fastened at the mortised joints with wooden pegs, then reinforced with handmade nails.[118] The original site of the house is still uncertain, although it may have been on what was then known as "Quality Hill"; Rice moved it to face on Court House Square from the north side, rightly judging that the city's business and social life would center there. He laid down floors of two-inch-thick longleaf pine and for much of the interior panelling, as well as the carved stair rail, insisted on that nineteenth-century favorite, rosewood.[119]

It can only be surmised whether Nichols drew up his plans himself or built what was known as a "pattern-book house." Architects were in short supply except in the largest cities of the East; there were in circulation all over the country a number of manuals giving details of doors, windows, mouldings, columns, and all the requisites of an elegant home, from which the prospective householder could pick what he liked and show it to his local builder. The house which took shape, in any event, is a fairly happy example of the Greek Revival, its front elevation presenting to the world a classic pediment supported by four Ionic columns, the whole divided by deep upper and lower galleries. A building of moderate size, it gives the impression of being higher than it actually is by the sweep of its windows; flanked by tall shutters, these may well have been intended for a house of quite different proportions. The interior, with Gulf Coast summers in mind, was arranged so that whatever breeze was about could move through all the rooms; folding doors between the downstairs parlors could be thrown back to create one spacious reception room running from the front of the house all the way through to the back. Kitchen and storerooms, as was the practice throughout the South, were set well away from the main house, as much to avoid heat, noise, and cooking smells as to reduce the danger of fire. Rice spent eight thousand dollars on finishing his residence, which in those days was considered a princely sum.[120]

Although the Abbé Domenech as late as July, 1848, could write somewhat testily in his account of "Missionary Adventures in Texas and Mexico" that "Houston is a wretched little town composed of about twenty shops and a hundred huts dispersed here and there among trunks of felled trees. It is infested with Methodists and ants,"[121] it is charitable to conclude that he was suffering from travel fatigue. While it is true that a gentleman who called himself Louis de France found few students when he opened a fencing school in Houston in the early eighteen-forties, one Emil Heerbrugger had more success at about the same time when he announced a concert featuring solos on the piano, the violin, and the French horn.[122] By 1845 the Houston Dramatic Society was affluent enough to present the mayor with thirty dollars toward "the relief of the indigent of the city and county,"[123] and although Houstonians had to wait until after Appomattox for opera and vaudeville, by 1859 Mr. and Mrs. William Marsh Rice might have been among those who gathered to hear a program of songs by Jenny Lind.[124] Professor Gillett had opened his Houston Academy as early as 1844, promising to teach "all branches necessary to enter any college in the United States" and by 1857 there were ten private schools doing a brisk business in the city, although the demand still far outran the supply.[125]

Like his father, William Marsh Rice did not shirk his responsibilities within the community of which he was a member. Christened in Springfield in the Methodist chapel so closely associated with David Rice, he seems in Houston to have become a member of the Episcopalian Christ Church soon after

its establishment, perhaps because Ebenezer Nichols and his
family as well as Margaret Bremond and her mother and sister
were all staunch Episcopalians.[126] For a number of years Christ
Church had to struggle to remain alive, and William Marsh
Rice's name appears regularly if prudently as one of those who
came to its financial rescue. In 1848 he was down in a subscription list in the amount of $40[127] toward paying off the church's
debts and a little later put up $10 toward the purchase of a
"melodeon" or "American organ," as the instrument was sometimes called.[128] When the question was raised of building a rectory, Frederick Allyn Rice, who had apparently followed his
brother into the Episcopal fold, contributed $50; William made
his contribution in a way that was equally effective and in
thorough keeping with the character of the man: "For my subscription to building of a Rectory for Christ Church I give and
release my interest in the indebtedness of the Church to Rice
and Nichols, excepting such amount as may be due on account
of the Cemetery."[129] Like Bremond & Van Alstyne, Rice &
Nichols gave $2 in 1848 toward decorating the church for "the
Christmas holly days"; the two firms thereby became the largest
contributors in that particular cause, representing one end of a
scale that diminished to a low of thirty cents.[130] During the Civil
War, when currency in Texas had become less reliable than
ever, William M. Rice was among those able to make a contribution to the rector's salary in specie.[131]

Through his association with Christ Church, Rice would have
seen a good deal at this time of a man whose name is intimately
bound up with the whole history of the Episcopal Church in
Texas, the Reverend Charles Gillette. Gillette, like David Rice,
worked tirelessly all his life in the cause of education and
through him William Marsh Rice must have become aware of
Houston's need for more and better schools. Before his congregation had a church in which to worship, Gillette had seen to
it that they had a schoolhouse, buying a frame building at
second hand and moving it onto the church's property at Texas
Avenue and Fannin Street, where it served as a parish hall
whenever need arose, for Sunday school and services on week-

ends, and where the rector started a day school during the week on his own initiative.[132] Having been exposed to the views of two men like David Rice and Charles Gillette, it is not surprising that William Marsh Rice's name appeared in 1856 as an incorporator of the Houston Academy, in 1857 as a member of the board of the Houston Educational Society, and, two years later, as a trustee of both the Second Ward Free School and the Texas Medical College.[133] The idea of a university had not yet entered the thoughts of most Houstonians; those young men who went on to college were sent back to the East even after the Civil War, as was the case with William Marsh Rice II, Frederick's second son and Rice's namesake, whose years at Princeton University were a gift from his uncle.[134]

Politics and public office seemed to lie outside the range of Rice's interests, although as far back as 1845 he had served on a committee on resolutions in a public meeting that approved the annexation of Texas to the United States.[135] Patriotism, however, never triumphed over prudence; the Texas Treasury Papers contain Rice and Nichols' letter to the Secretary in December of that same year pointing out that admission to the United States was not without its pitfalls.

> As the time for annexation approaches we find we are materially injured in our business in consequence of the risque we are compelled to take in keeping up our stock of goods . . . in view of which we would ask from you an order to the Collector at Galveston or instructions to him to deliver to us all American goods consigned to our address remaining in the custom House at the time [the] U. S. takes possession . . . . We ask this, that we may be placed on an equality with the *Yankees* who will bring in goods after annexation and sell in competition with us, who have paid duties in Texas.[136]

For two transplanted New Englanders this was strong language.

The New England cast of mind may also have been responsible for the fact that William Marsh Rice seems to have felt none of that enthusiasm for the Mexican War that seized upon so many Southerners and slaveholders. The campaigns of 1846 and 1847 which culminated in the American occupation of

Mexico City on September 14, 1847, were no doubt inevitable in view of the geographical and political pressures upon the United States government but Rice, ever the most practical of men, once more left military glory to those who cared for that sort of thing and went on attending to his own affairs. A life-long admirer of Sam Houston, Rice twice attached his name to letters asking that Houston address the citizenry, and from 1855 to 1857 he intermittently represented the Second Ward as an Alderman in the Houston City Council.[137] An Odd Fellow as well as a Mason, he was called to petit juries and to the Harris County grand jury; he served for one year on the slave patrol and for another with Liberty Fire Company No. 2138.[138] For this last, in 1852, he joined with some of the other businessmen of the city in getting together $200 for a Hummelman hand fire engine which was sent down from Boston.[139]

Margaret Bremond Rice remains almost invisible throughout these years, as was to be expected in an age when ladies' names appeared in print only when they married and when they were buried. In 1860 it was reported that on the occasion when Hook and Ladder Company No. 1 was presented with a new banner worked for them by the ladies of Houston, the firemen marched, in full uniform and with their "truck dressed," to the Rice home on Courthouse Square, where Mrs. Rice delivered the banner to W. Browne Botts and he made the presentation on behalf of the ladies.[140] Some fifty years after Margaret Rice's death, a Houston newspaper recalled the New Year's Day reception which was held each year on the ground floor of her home, the folding doors set open to their full extent and a long table, at which Mrs. Rice poured coffee for her guests, placed beneath the far windows of the room. As night fell, there was dancing;[141] like the strollers on the square, one sees Margaret Rice through the lighted windows for an instant and then she is gone.

In the census of 1860, William Marsh Rice was listed as being worth $750,000 in real and personal property, which may have made him the second richest man in Texas, second only to John Hunter Herndon of Brazoria County, a sugar planter whose wealth lay principally in land and slaves. The building which housed the firm of Rice and Nichols was one of the largest in Houston, three stories tall and a hundred feet deep.[142] Rice was involved in nearly every major business enterprise in the city and, along the way, had amicably dissolved his partnership with Ebenezer Nichols, whose interests now centered entirely in Galveston. Although as far back as 1849 the Deed Records of Brazoria County had recorded that William M. Rice and Charles W. Adams, "Merchants of Galveston," had contracted to supply sugar-making machinery and the material for a sugar house to one James Love at Oyster Creek plantation,[143] Rice seems always to have judged that, of the two cities, Houston held the greater promise. Adams was a New Hampshire man who had landed in Galveston in 1838 with a cargo of lumber from Bangor, Maine, and by 1858 he could claim that his ship, the *Louisa Eaton,* had brought in the first cargo of coffee direct from Rio de Janeiro.[144] He and Rice remained lifelong friends, although their business partnership was apparently a brief one, and Adams' son, Charles, was one of William Marsh Rice's few regular callers in the last year or two of Rice's life.

The affiliation with Nichols had been a profitable one for both men; Rice was able to choose such new partners in the future as his own personal tastes directed, and he now set up the firm of Groesbeeck, Rice and Company. Abraham Groesbeeck was an old acquaintance, one whose name figures almost as frequently as Rice's own in the legal and financial transactions of the time; the "and Company" was young Frederick Allyn Rice, now his brother's full-fledged partner. Frederick's daughter Minnie was to recall in later years, writing to her uncle on New Year's Day of 1899, "It seems but yesterday I was a little girl and drove with you and Mr. Groesbeck [sic] or Mr. Ennis behind the white horses. You gentlemen would talk business and I would listen until tired."[145] Which of the gentlemen had suggested that they take Minnie for a ride and whose were the white horses? The records do not say.

With these new associates, as with his earlier ones, Rice's affairs prospered. In 1851, shortly after Nichols had gone down to Galveston, Rice had also set up a limited partnership with a

few businessmen who operated, like himself, from the head of
the bayou under the name of the Houston and Galveston Navigation Company.[146] By 1858 he was an owner of the brig *William
M. Rice* which made the run from Galveston to Boston to pick
up New England ice during the long Texas summers.[147] For the
well-to-do, life could indeed be very agreeable. "Almost
anything, useful or luxurious, could be bought in San Antonio,
Galveston, or other major towns. Everything arrived out of
Europe or the North, usually via New Orleans, and with heavy
mark-ups. Anyone with good money could purchase ice, jewel-
ry, finely made guns, drugs, clothing, cosmetics and good liquors."[148]

   In 1856 the name William M. Rice and Company appears for
the first time in the Deed Records of Harris County.[149] Abraham
Groesbeeck was no longer a partner and the "and Company"
was Frederick Rice, who was eventually to handle most of his
brother's business interests in and around Houston. Their ac-
quisition of land and its development went ahead steadily: on
June 24, 1859, William Marsh Rice sold a lot on the north side
of the Buffalo Bayou to the Hazard Powder Company of Connecticut and contracted to erect a powder magazine on it "for
said company."[150] The firm was already buying cotton from the
planters in the river bottom lands and seeing to its shipment
overland and by water; Rice took the next logical step on January 2, 1860, when, along with Groesbeeck, Ennis and some
dozen others, he became an incorporator in the Houston Cotton
Compress Company,[151] thereby putting the staple under the
same control all the way from the field to the cotton exchanges
of the world. Cannily, he was too shrewd to go into cotton
raising himself, subject as it was to the endless uncertainties of
labor, soil conditions, unstable markets, and the weather.

CHAPTER II

THE WAR YEARS AND THEIR SEQUEL

Of Rice's views on slavery nothing written has survived. Back in Springfield in the mid-1830's, that "peculiar institution" had been one of the issues most hotly debated in the discussion of Texas' proposed entry into the United States. At the Asbury Chapel a resolution had even been passed at the Methodists' Quarterly Conference in July, 1835, to "close the chapel to all lectures on colonization and abolition," but hotter heads prevailed and within a matter of days the Society voted to rescind the resolution, after which antislavery discussions raged on.[152] Whatever William Marsh Rice's sentiments may have been in Massachusetts, his actions reveal him to have been a realist first and last; as such, he could not ignore the economic facts of life in the Southwest.

> Southern capitalism took a different turn from that developed in the North. The Texas capitalist had two ingredients to work with, fresh lands and Negro slaves. Out of this land and forced labor he created new capital, which almost universally was reinvested in more land and more slaves . . . . Few, if any, of these New England migrants who succeeded—as lawyers, doctors, merchants, or overseers—failed to acquire Negroes and set themselves up as Southern gentlemen. This indicates that geography more than morality permitted the American North and West to escape the incubus of Negro slavery.[153]

The period covered by William Marsh Rice's life is recent enough to leave room for hope that some questions about him may still be answered. Did he and his father correspond about the issues of slavery and secession as war drew closer? Did David Rice, speaking for his Massachusetts abolitionist friends, raise issues that his son in Texas found hard to answer? All that is recorded is that William Marsh Rice was in fact a slaveowner; in the census of 1860 he is listed as owning fifteen Negroes,[154] some of whom he had acquired in default of payments, as he had some of his land holdings; others, the records show, he purchased outright. In 1847, against the sum of $889.58, one John Lewis of Montgomery County secured four slaves to the firm of Rice and Nichols;[155] in 1861, at the trust sale of Amanda, aged 17 years, Rice offered $1050 and purchased her.[156] Like a number of the others, Amanda was most likely one of Margaret Bremond Rice's house servants; there must also have been a need for slaves in the warehouses and on the wharves owned by Rice and his several partners. The *Democratic Telegraph and Texas Register* reported in March, 1851, that a Negro belonging to the firm of Rice and Nichols had been brought to Houston from Galveston with symptons of smallpox; a week later the paper followed up with the welcome news that there had been no further signs of the disease in the city.[157] In 1848 Rice made a gift of "Ellen, 17, light black, and her infant child, Louisa, about 1," to Frank Rice Nichols, Ebenezer Nichols' son, out of "the love and affection" which Rice felt for the little boy;[158] it is one of the few instances where Rice put his personal feelings in a written document, and, perhaps characteristically, even then in regard to a business transaction.

Over the protests of the aging Sam Houston, Texas voted itself out of the United States in March, 1861; it had already been admitted to the Confederacy which was being put together in Montgomery, Alabama.[159] Some young men, like Rice's nephew William A. Rice, one of those two sons whom David Rice had left behind in Massachusetts and who had joined his father and uncles in Texas in the early 1850's, had already gone back North.[160] This William, like his cousin of nearly the same name, had his uncle to thank for his education at Wilbraham Academy and at Suffield Institute, and the two remained friends, although in the ironic pattern that characterized this war the son enlisted in the 37th Massachusetts Volunteers while David, his father, was to become an officer in Hood's Brigade.[161]

Given the kind of hard-headed man that William Marsh Rice

always showed himself to be, it is only reasonable to suppose that he agreed with Sam Houston in seeing secession as a disaster. With a first-hand understanding of the North's infinitely greater resources of men and materiel, he must have suspected what the outcome of war would be. On November 14, 1860, six days after Lincoln's election, Rice had been a member of the committee on resolutions which, at a public meeting, urged Sam Houston to convene the legislature, a step which the old statesman refused to take. Accordingly, the anti-Unionists acted without him and unconstitutionally called a state convention which resulted in the vote in favor of secession.[162] Presumably Rice, like many others, had hoped that Houston, with the force of a lifetime of authority behind him, might be able to prevent this very thing; it is hard to imagine William Marsh Rice taking the opposing stand and demanding to leave the Union.

With the coming of war, business life in Texas underwent an almost immediate change. The building of railroads came to a halt and the flow of merchandise through the coastal cities slowed to a trickle. Even more than most southern states, Texas had imported nearly everything—from the guns on which the frontier's life depended to the very clothing worn by the slaves. It still held one trump card: cotton. Although the Gulf Coast came under a naval blockade within a few months of the fall of Fort Sumter,[163] at the outset the effect of this measure was negligible. Blockade runners found that profits outweighed risks and soon in the Mexican waters below Matamoros "foreign ships by the hundreds lay off the mouth of the Rio Grande, while their captains clamored for cargoes and bid the price of cotton to enormous sums."[164] The French and British warships at large in the Gulf of Mexico, ever on the lookout for Yankee infringement of the freedom of the seas, were of great help to the Confederates.

Even so, by December of 1861 trade had fallen off so much in Galveston that the firm of E. B. Nichols and Company moved back to Houston into the building owned by William Marsh Rice and Company, where, significantly, there was plenty of room for it.[165] Warehouses stood increasingly empty after

Galveston was seized by Federal forces in October, 1862, although Magruder captured it on the following New Year's
Day.[166] Goods that could be brought in through the blockade
commanded enormous prices. "A very fair estimate of actual
conditions in Houston about the middle years of the war would
be the following: General Magruder and his staff lived on the
fat of the land. Several favored and adventurous merchants
grew rich, honorably, by running the blockade. Dozens of army
contractors got rich, any old way."[167] Whether the "brig *William
M. Rice*" was among those running the blockade can only be
a matter for conjecture; certainly it has never been suggested
that her owner profited at the expense of the Confederate Government.

Margaret Bremond Rice, for her part, seems to have worked
tirelessly in what would now be called war relief, and her
husband's name appeared regularly on the lists of those who
contributed to various patriotic causes. On April 23, 1862,
"Wm. M. Rice and Company" gave $200 toward the purchase
of a home for the widow and children of Albert Sidney Johnston, dead on the battlefield at Shiloh;[168] on the sixth of June of
that same year, the firm gave $25 for the relief of volunteers'
families and on June 27th raised this to a monthly contribution
of $50.[169] In October, Margaret Rice contributed "5 blankets, 2
pairs drawers, 2 shirts to the soldiers,"[170] for the Confederacy
was already feeling the pinch of its lack of textile mills and by
Appomattox many of its soldiers were even wearing Yankee
cast-offs. During Christmas week of 1862, while Magruder was
making plans for his raid on Galveston, Margaret Rice, together
with a number of other ladies, arranged a concert for the benefit
of Hood's Brigade;[171] on New Year's Eve she was sent an additional $230 from Danville in Montgomery County and herself
added another $100 on January 6, 1863.[172]

Under Hood's command with the First Texas Regiment was
William Marsh Rice's brother David; a captain at the age of
forty-eight, he was finding himself at last. At Gettysburg and
Chickamauga he was to display conspicuous bravery under fire
and his regiment is mentioned several times in accounts which

show that the efforts of Margaret Rice and the ladies of Houston were made in response to real need. At Bean's Station in Tennessee, "on or about 16 December 1863," the brigadier commanding the Texans refused to advance when the order was given, claiming in the subsequent investigation that his men "had but three days rations on hand and God knows where more are to come from" and were marching without shoes, for all General Longstreet's promises.[173] Margaret Rice could no longer take up funds for the Texans, for by that December she was dead. The records of Christ Church show that her death took place on August 13, 1863, and that she was buried in the Episcopal Cemetery the following day by the Reverend Benjamin Eaton, who had married her to William Marsh Rice thirteen years before.[174] The cause of her death is not known; Rice never referred afterward to anything except the fact and the date in the documents that have so far come to light. But yellow fever and cholera appeared in Houston nearly every summer and the war years were no exception; medicines and even doctors were in critical shortage.

The Houston *Telegraph,* in an obituary notice which reflects to something of a fault the unrestrained sentimentality of the mid-nineteenth century, nonetheless conveys some idea of what must have been the first Mrs. Rice's graces.

> Mrs. Rice was the eldest daughter of Paul Bremond, Esq., and for the last fourteen years was a resident of this city. During that time she had, by her uniform kindness, affability of manners, and affectionate disposition, endeared herself to all who knew her; but, more especially was it her constant and disinterested kindness to the sick and afflicted that revealed her true character, and won the esteem and admiration of so many. During the epidemics that have desolated so many homes, she was a constant watcher—an administering angel—insensible to fatigue and exposure. Upon our sick and disabled soldiers, she was ever ready to bestow her sympathies, and many a manly breast has been cheered by her encouraging smiles and sisterly attentions, and by them many a grateful recollection will be cherished. Believing from the sorrowful countenances of those around her bedside that no hopes were entertained of her recovery, peacefully, and with christian resignation, she divested her mind of the allurements and concerns of this world,

and putting her temporal affairs in order, prepared for the brighter and happier one that her spirit longed for.[175]

Among the papers in the estate of William Marsh Rice there is a rather curious document relating to Margaret Rice's death, a handwritten statement dated May 6, 1867, which begins "To all whom it may concern." The writer is Dr. William McCraven, an old Houston friend of whom, according to McCraven's daughter, William Marsh Rice "was very fond."[176] In its entirety, the statement runs as follows:

I attended the late Margaret B. Rice, wife of Wm. M. Rice during the Latter part of her last illness. Two or three days, I think, before her death I was invited into her room, and found her alone with her husband. She informed me her husband had kindly assented to her leaving some legacies to her relations and friends, and that she wished me to be a witness to the same. She then, in her proper mind, proceeded to state clearly and distinctly her wishes, in the presence of her husband, devising to some specific sums of money and to others annuities for life—to all of which I understood her husband to give his full assent. When I left her later, at night, I was desired to call at judge Grays on my way home and desire him to call at Mr. Rices, as soon as convenient, to reduce her will to writing. He informed me afterwards that when he called they concluded not to have the writing executed. In the course of the next day I was informed that Mrs. Rice was laboring under great excitement and mental anguish, and declared that she could not die in her then condition of mind. I was informed that every one was excluded from the room but Mr. Rice, who was endeavouring to soothe and calm her. I was not admitted to her room that afternoon or night. On the next morning I found her calm and she continued comparatively so till her death.

What took place during the period of seclusion I have, of course, no personal knowledge—but every thing which I saw or heard—every thing which transpired in her presence tended to confirm what I afterwards learned she had communicated to her husband during this state of mental anguish. I have no hesitation in saying that this communication, in my judgment, wholly exonorated Mr. Rice from the obligations which he so cheerfully assumed to carry out the provisions of her will. I have no doubt she intended that the obligations should be cancelled. Taking all things into consideration I have no hesitation in affirming that Mr. Rice acted throughout the most trying affair with extreme delicacy and unsullied honour.

With the express sanction of Mr. Rice I mentioned the substance of what had happened to one of the parties most in interest who seemed fully to assent to the proposition that it totally absolved Mr. Rice from all obligation to carry out the will. The party concerned seemed neither to question the *facts* of the case or the *justice* of the *conclusion.* Upon a full and impartial view of the whole matter I think Mr. Rice not only justified in refusing to carry out the provisions of the will, but that he could not consent to do so without dishonour. He has acted in a most delicate affair with great propriety . . . [illegible] and judgment.

Wm. McCraven[177]

There seems to be a deliberate attempt here not to make explicit the precise nature of this situation; nonetheless it is apparent that William Marsh Rice met a difficult situation with considerable insight and understanding. He chose, however, not to remain long in Houston; by early December, while David Rice marched hungry in Tennessee and only Galveston and Sabine Pass, of all the Texas Gulf ports, were still in Confederate hands,[178] Rice had crossed the Mexican border on his way south to Monterrey.[179]

Between December, 1863, and August, 1865, Rice's movements are almost impossible to follow. On December 8 he drew up a will leaving everything he possessed to his brother, Frederick Allyn Rice, who was also named as executor.[180] Immediately afterwards, entering Mexico, he plunged into one of the most confused areas, politically, militarily, and financially, of any Civil War theater of operations. Only two documents are known relating to Rice during these twenty months, one being a laconic handwritten receipt dated July 17, 1865:

Received at Matamoros Mexico, of Wm. M. Rice, Esqre., for a/c of T. C. Armstrong Esqre. of Galveston Texas the sum of Fifty dollars in coin.

Frank T. L'Estrange[181]

The second document relating to this period is a draft in Rice's own handwriting now found among the William Marsh Rice papers in the Fondren Library of Rice University of a statement which was probably to be used in preparing Rice's suit over his second wife's will. The relevant paragraph reads:

The war broke up my business. In August 1863 my first wife died and in the December following I went to Mexico—Monteray and down to Matamoros and after a little delay on to Havana, remained there a month or two, then returned to Matamoros where I was in business until August 1865, at which time I returned to Houston.[182]

The situation on both sides of the lower Rio Grande Valley in the last years of the war was an unstable and sometimes farcical one, involving not only the Confederate and Union forces who were maneuvering for control of Brownsville from the sea as well as from the land, but also the two elements then at war in Mexico plus the support which had been sent to the conservative wing by Napoleon III to shore up his dreams of empire. The Confederate government, not to mention the entire South, saw the situation above all else in terms of cotton: only if the cumbersome bales kept moving toward the Gulf ports could the fast-emptying treasury at Richmond be replenished. The harbors of Georgia and the Carolinas had been effectively closed by the Union blockade. Not even Rice and Paul Bremond could have foreseen how desperate the need for railroads would come to be at a time like this: as things were, the cotton had to be "carried in wagon trains to some central point, usually San Antonio or Goliad, and from there to Brownsville, Laredo, or Eagle Pass."[183] "The haul from the Colorado to the border was long, arduous, and expensive; there were only trails through the chaparral. But the brush country was white with falling cotton lint, because the fiber sold for a dollar, gold, per pound."[184]

Arrived at the mouth of the Rio Grande, the cotton was carried by blockade runners or "neutral" vessels (Richard King and Mifflin Kenedy transferred their river steamers to friendly Mexican ownership at about this time),[185] to ports in Cuba and the Bahamas whence they were transshipped to the textile mills of New England as well as those of Liverpool.

With his usual acuteness, William Marsh Rice had managed to be where the money was waiting. "Brownsville swelled to about 25,000 and Matamoros to 40,000. Bagdad on the Rio [the port city for Matamoros on the south side of the entrance to the

Rio Grande] exploded to 15,000. The population was polyglot, with peddlers, merchants, deserters, gamblers, swindlers, undercover agents, and whores from a dozen nations. Times were flush; a number of merchants made immense fortunes from the cotton trade. Common laborers earned $5 to $10 daily, paid in good silver . . . . Lightermen could make $40 a day. There is no record of how much prostitution and swindling paid. But millions in gold passed through all three towns."[186] Gold is something all governments respect; William Marsh Rice, who had gone into the war a rich man, was one of those who came out of it even wealthier. He interpreted the handwriting on the wall correctly: in April, 1864, a year before Appomattox, he instructed Frederick to have the entire stock of William M. Rice and Company sold in Houston at public outcry.[187] It would have been a long time before any of the firm's subsequent customers could have paid in anything but Confederate money—or promissory notes.

The last battle of the Civil War was fought more than a month after Lee's surrender, outside of Brownsville at Palmito Hill, in May, 1865. Within three months Rice was back in Houston and again actively involved in the business life of that city, for by September 19, 1865, the City Council had granted his petition to add another story to the Post Office building "or to raise the roof."[188] The Houston of Reconstruction, however, had changed from the Houston of the prewar years. With the collapse of the agrarian South, helped on by the wartime Currency Acts, more and more of the country's wealth was controlled from New York, and with the same acumen that had taken him out of Massachusetts at the close of the 1830's, William Marsh Rice made the decision to return north. His nephew William A. Rice, the same who had served with the 37th Massachusetts Volunteers, did indeed suggest forty years later that his uncle was suspected in Texas of Northern sympathies and so found it more prudent to carry on his postwar business in Houston through agents.[189] Given Rice's business insight, it is more likely that the eastward flight of capital plus the fact that his warehouses and other premises had been taken over as barracks and storage depots by the United States government[190] prompted the move. Conditions all along the Gulf Coast were in a state of disorganization, with few signs that better times would come soon.

William Marsh Rice went almost at once to Palmer, Massachusetts, where his father and mother, whom he had not seen since the outbreak of the war, were then living. This, in the late summer of 1865, was the first of the yearly visits he was to make from then on, always with some sort of gift.[191] To his parents he announced that New York was henceforth to be his home; that "he could get interest on his deposits in New York more promptly than he could in Texas"; that Confederate bonds were worthless and furthermore that "he could not collect his debts in Texas."[192] William A. Rice, still speaking of his uncle, made an observation which must have occurred to many people: he was "reticent in talking about his property."

Rice's business ties to Texas, however, were still strong; by January, 1866, he was back in Houston and caught up in the thick of things. On June 7 the Houston Insurance Company, which had been chartered just before the outbreak of the war, was reorganized with Rice as a director; perhaps with the memory of his own youthful losses still clearly in mind, it provided for "insurance on ships and freights from navigation or fire; upon railroad cars and goods carried by them; against fire in transit; upon buildings, wares from fire; to lend money."[193] By October of that same year the Houston Direct Navigation Company had its charter extended for another year and undertook "to improve bayou over Red Fish Bar and between mouth of bayou and Galveston Harbor";[194] by 1869, with William Marsh Rice remaining on the board of directors, it had been superseded by the Buffalo Bayou Ship Channel Company which guaranteed nine feet of water at all times from the Bolivar Channel all the way to Houston.[195]

The charter of this last company contained the significant phrase, "To receive grants of lands as do railroads," for in March of 1868, Rice, together with two other shrewd directors of the Houston and Texas Central, had set up a partnership for laying out the townsites along the route of the expanding railroad. "In their capacities as directors of the company, they knew where the railroad was going and when it would be built to any given point, so there was little difficulty about their laying out a multitude of railhead towns for the period that the railroad ended in them."[196] Characteristically, Rice made no attempt to get back into the cotton business on a large scale; the once inexhaustible supply of black labor which had made nearly the entire lower South dependent on a single crop was no more. Rice, with his very solid wartime profits, looked elsewhere.

Houston was in any case no longer his headquarters. In the summer of 1866 he had been back in Palmer, informing his sister Charlotte of his intention to buy a home for their parents in Three Rivers, Massachusetts; by November the property was his and David and Patty Hall Rice moved in on the sixth of that month, along with Charlotte, her husband Collins McKee, and their children.[197] Like other childless men, Rice gave a good deal of thought to his relatives, sending up from New York during the following summer the "carpets and chamber sets" which his sisters remembered. Charlotte seems to have shared her brother's extraordinary memory for detail, for, forty years after that summer, she mentioned no less than three times the set of silver spoons which he had promised her and which never arrived.[198]

Their father, David Rice, died in March, 1867, after less than six months in the new house; in June of that year William Marsh Rice amended his will, leaving ten thousand dollars to each of his surviving sisters, Louisa, Charlotte, and Minerva. The income was to be theirs during their lifetimes and the principal thereafter passed to their children.[199] None of the three had made, in a financial sense, a particularly successful marriage, and Louisa Rice Blinn's may have been a domestic disaster as well. Writing to thank Charlotte for her birthday congratulations in the spring of 1899, Rice made one of the occasional confidences of his old age.

Blinn was such a rough man. I do not see how Louisa lived as long as she did—whilst she was affectionate and kind. [Louisa, the oldest of David and Patty Rice's children, married Lathrop Blinn in 1830 at the age of 18 and died in 1877.[200]] He was abusive and the longer he lived the worse he got. I suppose it was the result of his parentage and the people he was raised amongst. Louisa had plenty of offers but did not fancy them. Blinn was a very handsom [sic] fellow. He earned big wages at his trade but he was afraid to use it—for a long time he carried it about in a little pretty box—and used to take it out and count.[201]

Louisa's one child, a son, Joseph, later claimed that his uncle William, "the Texas millionaire," was accustomed to send him $300 from Texas every Christmas "because he knew he would make good use of it."[202] Far more in character is the story that when young Joseph's wife offered to return the $500 Uncle William had sent her toward setting up her millinery business, she received the answer, "No one of my relatives ever did send me any money and you'd better not."[203]

Eight days after signing this will of 1867, on the morning of June 26, William Marsh Rice was married at Christ Church in Houston for the second time; he was fifty-one and his bride, Julia Elizabeth Baldwin Brown, was a widow some twelve years younger.[204] The summer of 1867 brought with it the worst yellow fever epidemic in Houston's history; nearly five hundred people were to die before the year was out, including eight doctors and a considerable number of Union troops still quartered in the city.[205] Immediately after the ceremony Mr. and Mrs. Rice prudently left for the East.[206]

Julia Elizabeth Baldwin—who apparently never used her first given name and preferred the "Libbie" that harked back to her childhood—was a younger sister of that Charlotte Baldwin Randon who had also been widowed at the time of her marriage to Frederick Allyn Rice in 1854. Elizabeth Baldwin had come out to Texas from Baldwinsville, New York, at around the age of twelve; within a few years her father, Horace Baldwin, was to become mayor of Houston and her aunt, Charlotte Baldwin Allen, held an undisputed position in society as the wife of one of the city's founders.[207] Something quite brilliant might have been expected of Elizabeth Baldwin in the way of a match, but on July 4, 1847, she married John H. Brown, who seems to have been unremarkable in every way.[208] "A shopkeeper [who] held a series of minor political offices," Brown "never acquired any substance other than a few tracts of wild lands in Texas";[209] after the discovery of gold in California he and his wife moved to San Francisco, where he no doubt looked forward to better luck.[210] A haberdashery shop was apparently the best he could do and in 1862 the Browns moved from Oakland back to New York, where he died in 1866 after having "lost everything he had."[211]

In that same year William Marsh Rice had finished with one phase of his life and was starting out on another. After spending the early part of the winter in New York, he was back in Houston in January, collecting debts still outstanding from the early war years. At the same time he leased to W. B. Hamblin the "Eastern Office room in one story brick building recently erected fronting on Congress Street and opposite the Court House Square" for an annual payment of three hundred dollars in gold[212] and spent a considerable amount of time over the affairs of the Galveston ship channel company. The late summer of 1866 found him once again in Massachusetts, negotiating the purchase of the Three Rivers house. Elizabeth Baldwin Brown must have been an old acquaintance, both by reason of the marriage of her sister to his brother and through the fact that Rice acted as John H. Brown's agent as far back as 1859, when he handled the sale of some property in Houston and a slave, Henry, for Brown, who was then in San Francisco.[213] Rice and Elizabeth Brown renewed their friendship during the winter of 1866-1867 after Brown's death. Brown's "widow was without means, and came to Houston in the fall of 1866 hoping to find some property they had left in Texas, but she found only some wild land which was unsaleable and produce[d] but a trifle. When she arrived she went to the home of her sister, Mrs. F. A. Rice, and spent some time with her Aunt Mrs. A. C. Allen. She was dependent and unhappy and took charge of the house of Judge Shearn, who had a young adopted daughter."[214]

Controversy was to go on for years over the character of the second Mrs. William Marsh Rice. James Baker described her on a public occasion much later as "a brilliant woman, unusually handsome, tall and straight as an Indian. Nature favored her with wondrous eyes and a handsome suit of hair . . . .She loved people and was always happiest when doing for others."[215]

In private conversation, the attorney was less generous. "She was a very ambitious woman; . . . she was fond of society and she was fond of being in the public eye."[216] Like Rice himself, Elizabeth Baldwin had remained childless during her first marriage; a wealthy widower, Rice might have taken his pick of any number of Houston's young belles but he chose instead this sister-in-law whose tastes were to be so incompatible with his own. Being of an imperious nature, perhaps she chose him. In any event, judging by the subsequent testimony of relatives and friends, he seems always to have treated her with unfailing, if unyielding, affection and courtesy.

After a few days at a hotel in New York, William Marsh Rice and his bride went on to stay for several weeks at "some springs on the borders of Canada."[217] On this occasion, as later, the second Mrs. Rice was not taken to visit her husband's relatives in Massachusetts; Patty Hall Rice had made it so plain to everyone that she did not care to meet this new daughter-in-law that on all of Rice's subsequent visits to Three Rivers, even after his mother's death in 1877, he came alone.

Mention is first made at about this time of that increasing preoccupation with the state of his own health which was to characterize William Marsh Rice's later years. His Unionist nephew, William A. Rice, had married some time during the winter of 1866; his bride appears to have been in frail health the following summer when Uncle William visited with them briefly and strongly urged the young woman to take "some pills" out of the supply of medicines which he always kept by him.[218] Whether this incipient hypochondria influenced his choice of a health resort for his 1867 wedding trip is a moot point; "going to the springs," in the United States as on the Continent, had for a long time been as much a social function as a medical one. The Rices that season could have enjoyed saline-sulphur baths at Massena in New York, as well as a prospect of the Raquette

River and a drive to the neighboring Indian village of St. Regis, or, not far away, "on the Canadian border" at Sheldon or Alburg Springs they might have taken advantage of the alkaline waters and the splendid view of Lake Champlain.[219]

Whatever their preference may have been, they returned to New York early in the fall and moved into a suite of rooms at the Union Square Hotel,[220] the first of several such installations in the city. Rice may even then have had it in mind to settle down somewhere away from the center of New York but not too far for him to be able to watch over every detail of his business interests. By the following January he had been called back to Texas to look into his investments there; Elizabeth Baldwin Rice accompanied him and they remained in Houston, at the home of the Frederick Allyn Rices, "until warm weather came."[221]

After Margaret Bremond's death, William Marsh Rice never again lived in the Greek Revival house on Court House Square, and in 1871 or 1872 it "was sold, together with his other property in the same block, to the Houston Savings Bank."[222] For the remainder of his life, with the exception of the five years from 1873 to 1878 when he was engrossed in the improvements he was making to his farm in New Jersey,[223] it was the Rices' habit to avoid the Gulf Coast summer weather by returning to New York, which he always spoke of as his residence, in May or June, and remaining there until cold weather closed in, when they would again remove to Houston. When they did not stay with Frederick and Charlotte Baldwin Rice, they would usually spend the winter months with such old friends as the Groesbeecks or the Timpsons. Society at that time in most Southern cities was characterized by a labyrinth of intermarriages, and Houston was no exception; Margaret Bremond's sister, Harriet, had married Samuel Timpson and their son, Paul Bremond Timpson, in the 1890's was to marry Frederick Allyn Rice's youngest daughter, Lottie.[224]

There is evidence that Elizabeth Baldwin Rice was not altogether satisfied with this peripatetic style of life; freed of financial anxieties for the first time, she began to enlarge her social ambitions. As late as 1894, when Charles Shearn's granddaughter wished to sell her "handsome home on Main Street" in Houston, Mrs. Rice still apparently cherished the hope that her husband would acquire a substantial residence in that city. The house was "nicely arranged for entertaining" and would have, in addition, gratified Mr. Rice's predisposition for plenty of fresh air.[225] William Marsh Rice disappointed both owner and prospective buyer by stating flatly that he had no wish to be encumbered with a place of that size for the few months of the year that he spent in Texas. The idea of launching out on a giddy round of entertainment can hardly have held much appeal for a retiring man of seventy-eight.

With the arrival of the summer heat of 1868 and the "musketoes" which both Rices found so trying,[226] they returned to New York, stopping at the St. Nicholas Hotel on Broadway.[227] By early winter he was again at his brother's house in Houston, but Elizabeth Baldwin Rice elected to remain behind in New York this time, at "a boarding house where she had lived with her former husband."[228] The urgency of business, however, kept Rice on in Texas into the summer months and she came out to join him some time in June or July, remaining until they returned to New York together "towards the end of the year."[229]

The "urgent business" that kept Rice in Houston may well have been connected with the death of the Houston and Texas Central Railroad's financial agent in New York City. Rice, who had been one of the company's directors from the first, solved the problem by taking over the position himself and keeping it, with its offices at 52 Wall Street, until the road was sold out in 1877 to Charles Morgan of New Orleans.[230] When in New York, the Rices continued to live either at the Pierrepont House, a "family hotel" in Brooklyn, or at other places of its kind in different parts of the city[231] until, in the early spring of 1872, their way of life underwent a profound change.

Remarriage and the fact that he was spending at least a part of each year in the Southwest had not loosened William Marsh Rice's ties to his kin in Massachusetts; he kept up a fairly regular correspondence with his sisters and his mother and continued to help them out financially. However, as early as 1870, to the best of Charlotte Rice McKee's recollection, he spoke of buying a place in New Jersey where he could spend the summers and he asked her if she "would like to go and take charge of it."[232] Charlotte's husband, Collins McKee, whom she had married in 1851, gave his occupation at that time as a carriage maker,[233] but he appears to have had only moderate success at it. After David Rice's death in 1867, McKee and Charlotte and their children continued to live with Patty Rice at Three Rivers, a state of affairs which may not have been entirely satisfactory. William Marsh Rice seems to have been geniunely fond of Charlotte and he must already have realized that winters in the New Jersey countryside would hold small charm for his own wife.

True to his lifelong principles, Rice said nothing to anyone and left no written explanation of his reasons for settling on Somerset County, New Jersey. Presumably he had determined some limit beyond which he was not prepared to commute regularly to his New York offices; the little town of Dunellen, on the Central Railroad of New Jersey, is just under thirty miles from Manhattan. Crossing from Wall Street on the Liberty Street ferry, Rice would have had a choice at that time of nineteen trains out from the city on weekdays and three on Sundays.[234]

The result was that on October 7, 1871, one Robert Lourie, or Lowrie, and his wife, Susan, sold to Collins and Charlotte McKee, of Hampden County, Massachusetts, three tracts of land totalling just over one hundred acres for $16,000, to secure a part of which the Louries took a mortgage of $9,500 on the property.[235] Charlotte McKee remembered in 1904 that the deed had been "taken out in the name of my husband and myself,"[236] but it can be safely assumed that William Marsh Rice put up the actual cash which changed hands. After Collins McKee's death this property, plus an additional eight acres sold by the Louries to the McKees shortly afterward, was valued at $16,400, subject to the abovementioned mortgage, of which $6,500 was due to William Marsh Rice.[237]

In later years Rice always spoke of having resided at Dunellen, New Jersey, but his estate lay about two miles beyond that village—then composed principally of the railroad station, the post office, and "two or three stores"[238]—at an even smaller settlement called Green Brook. Whatever the practical advantages of the site may have been, William Marsh Rice had an eye for a pretty bit of countryside; the property lies below a chain of hills, in an area characterized by many kinds of hardwoods and numerous small streams—not unlike, in some ways, the country around Springfield, Massachusetts, but more open and with a lighter, sandier soil. Thirty years later, there were still people around to remember the "old farm house" which stood on the place when the McKees moved there in March, 1872.[239]

Collins McKee seems to have been one of those men for whom bad luck is second nature; three weeks after his arrival in New Jersey he died of pneumonia, on March 23, at the early age of 44.[240] William Marsh Rice came out from New York to attend his brother-in-law's funeral and brought Elizabeth Baldwin Rice with him; it was the first time that the sisters-in-law had met.[241]

In later testimony Charlotte Rice McKee revealed herself to be the possessor of a sound memory and strong opinions; it is to be regretted that those who were taking testimony in the litigation over Elizabeth Baldwin Rice's will did not question the one lady more specifically about the other. The facts are simply that the Rices remained on at Green Brook after the funeral was over and did not take up residence in New York again until 1883, eleven years later. "He said it would be more restful than living in [the] city as he enjoyed being out in the country all he could."[242] When the McKees moved in, there were a number of outbuildings standing on the Green Brook property in addition to the farm house: a barn, a "cow hovel," wagon and wood sheds, and several corn cribs.[243] Remodelling had been started on the old house, but when William Marsh Rice decided to make New Jersey his residence the year around, he did not do things by halves. Only one problem allowed from the first of no solution: the presence under one roof of two strong-minded women. Less than twelve months after she had arrived, Charlotte Rice McKee and her children went back to Massachusetts. "I left there because I did not want to stay there any longer," was the only statement she ever made regarding this period,[244] but a friend who had known both Rices since her own Houston childhood and who visited with them in New Jersey during the 1870's (Mary Emma Todd), remembered overhearing William Marsh Rice make the statement that his sister had left "because Mrs. Rice did not like her."[245]

It took more than domestic differences to distract Rice from business. On September 2, 1872, he paid Charlotte McKee $2,000 for her interest in the four tracts of land, and, on the grounds that the estate owed him $6,500—the original sum of cash which had been put up towards its purchase—bought up her deceased husband's share of the property at public venue for $2,600 thirteen months later.[246] In all fairness it must be said that he never seems to have considered Green Brook purely as a business speculation, but rather as a permanent home for himself, just as he must once have looked upon the Court House Square property in Houston.

"Large enough to live in," commented the architect who was asked to make a drawing, many years later, of the house which William Marsh Rice had built for himself in the mid-'seventies, "and [a] house large enough to live in is large enough to die in."[247] Because of a few fine trees which had stood around the old farmhouse, the new "gentleman's country residence"[248] which rose to take its place was situated only a few hundred yards away. The foundations were of stone and brick "of [the] best material and [the] best workmanship"[249] and on the basement level there were a large kitchen, a still larger laundry room, a furnace room and cellar for storage, and a wine-cellar stretching ten feet by twenty-four feet—although he eschewed alcohol himself, William Marsh Rice did not intend that his guests should go thirsty. The first floor was laid out in a number of reception rooms; wide stairs led up from a covered carriage entrance through a foyer and spacious hall to a parlor looking out over terraces on two sides. The library and dining room, each with its open fireplace, adjoined this and meals were brought up from the kitchen in a dumb waiter, except during the summer months when all of the cooking went on in a separate kitchen built of brick at some distance from the main house. On the second floor were three large bedrooms, the most imposing of which opened on to a wide balcony and was flanked by a dressing-room nearly as large as it was. Five more rooms, all of a respectable size, made up the third floor, but the house servants lived in separate quarters, complete with their own kitchen.[250] The main house itself was built of clapboard and cypress shingle, painted grey and swelling out into arbitrary ells and bays, with what a country neighbor described as a "French roof" and was undoubtedly mansard. High above all rose a mansarded cupola, where William Marsh Rice liked to sit and watch his men at their work.[251]

Rice was approaching sixty. His years as a merchant and businessman had made him extremely wealthy and with wise management of his investments that wealth could not fail to increase. Notwithstanding two marriages he was childless and likely to remain so, although for many years he had found satisfaction in looking after the welfare of his brothers and sisters and an increasing number of nieces and nephews. After Charlotte's return to Massachusetts with her children, he continued to send her monthly checks up to the time of his death—a period of some twenty-seven years.[252] He had no desire to cut a wide swathe in society, to gamble, to go on the Grand Tour, or to spend large sums on what he ate and drank. What he proceeded to do, with every evidence of satisfaction, was to put a great deal of money into his new country place.

In many respects, this must have been one of the happiest periods of Rice's life. Growing up in a New England manufacturing town, moving on to the constantly changing scene of the Southwest and returning again to New York City and an existence divided between Wall Street and a series of hotel rooms, he came late to country living knowing what he liked and with almost unlimited means to procure it. From the unpaved road that ran by his property and along which one drove from the railroad station at Dunellen, he laid out a circular carriage drive to his new home, macademized it, and set maple trees along both sides.[253] To screen his property from the gaze of the curious, he planted a hedge of lignum vitae beside the highway itself. As if to emphasize how permanent he expected his residence to be, Rice had his outbuildings and dependencies put up with unusual care. "First Class means a good deal," he was to admonish his Houston business agent less than a year before his death; "First Class is the best."[254] The carriage house and connecting stables were built over deep cellars and on stone foundations, as was the wagon shed, and the stableyard itself was laid off with walls of the same stone. Besides the cattle barns, hay lofts, and corncribs, there was a one-story "hennery" of brick and an octagonal brick smokehouse that boasted a "highly improved style of ventilation."[255] Against the hill behind his house Rice built a reservoir and ice house, bringing out laborers from Castle Garden to mix cement and break stone, and piped the water down to his house and barns. Under the summer kitchen there was a brick milk room, where the milk pans stood in a shallow sluice and were constantly cooled by running water.[256]

William Marsh Rice may have had in mind the plantations of the Gulf Coast when he laid out an orchard of apple and pear trees and planted vines as well as a kitchen garden, from which he provisioned his own household and the households of his farm workers. At Green Brook there were usually eight or ten milch cows and Rice not only raised his own hay but oats, corn, rye, wheat, and potatoes as well. Hams and bacon came from the smokehouse to the Rices' table and the "hennery" produced enough chickens and eggs for him to market the surplus. Sometimes one of his workmen drove the farm wagon into Plainfield and made the round of local merchants, but more often it was Rice himself who got into the buggy and carried eggs to the neighboring stores.[257] Besides the buggy and the farm wagon, at the "Green Brook Villa" the Rices kept a phaeton and two carriages.

For the first five or six years after his move out to Somerset County, Rice spent very little time away; his name appears less frequently on the deed and mortgage records of Harris and the neighboring counties than it had for many years. An hour's train ride took him to Wall Street and the affairs of the Houston and Texas Central Railroad, which by 1874 was able to boast that "Pullman Palace Drawing-Room and Sleeping Cars Run Through from Texas to St. Louis Without Change, And With But One Change To New York and Other Large Cities in the East";[258] afternoons found him back at Green Brook. Both he and Elizabeth Baldwin Rice seem for a time to have taken a fancy to raising horses and even brought one mare up from Texas,[259] which promptly ran away at the sight of a flapping clothesline and threw Rice out of the buggy.[260]

The same neighbor who remembered this a quarter of a century later also remarked that Rice did not know how to drive a horse "good enough," but, like most of the inhabitants of Dunellen, he accepted this newcomer from Texas both as a man and as a neighbor. Local workmen found jobs at Green Brook setting out fruit trees and shrubs, clipping the screening hedges from muleback, getting in hay, and shelling corn. They all mentioned the fact that William Marsh Rice liked to walk over his property and talk with them about the work that was going on, sometimes lending a hand himself, although he did not do this as often after he was caught and injured in the cogs of the corn sheller.[261] The neighbors expressed very little curiosity about him. "He went off on business, used to tell me he had business in New York,"[262] was the general impression, although it was understood from the first that Mr. Rice was a man who liked to get his money's worth; a man that "wanted you to work hard. If a man did not do that, he had no use for him."[263] They could approve of this. "He wanted everything done first class,"[264] volunteered one of his farm workers, and the caretaker added, "If I wanted anything for the place he would never hesitate in getting it; he was liberal that way."[265]

Meanwhile Elizabeth Baldwin Rice, although described by James Baker and others as a woman anxious to make a place for herself in society, seems at Green Brook to have gone out of her way to keep on good terms with her unsophisticated neighbors. Herman Trust's three young daughters, who lived across from the Green Brook Villa, remembered running in and out of the Rices' house all day long; the eldest, Josephine, used to help Mrs. Rice about the house when she was without servants, who were difficult to find and to keep at that distance from the city.[266] "Feenie," as both Rices called her, considered Mrs. Rice "a kind woman" and "a very truthful person," and all three sisters spoke of how "kindly" and "nicely" she behaved toward her husband and he to her.[267] Charles Carpenter, the stationmaster at Dunellen, and his wife Isabel, were considered friends by the Rices; Isabel Carpenter recalled that "sometimes Mrs. Rice would come to my house and invite me to go there saying 'I want you to go home with me.' [She] would come in [the] morning sometimes and ask me home with her and keep me all day."[268] When the Carpenters' second child was born, Elizabeth Baldwin Rice asked to have it named after her and presented Isabel Carpenter with elaborately embroidered baby clothes; disappointed that the infant turned out to be a boy, she then rather thoughtlessly suggested calling it William Rice Carpenter, which naturally caused a certain amount of gossip in the neighborhood.[269] Charles Carpenter recollected that once or twice when Mr. Rice was away on business, Mrs. Rice asked him to stay up at the big house at night; she did not like being alone there with only the servants.[270] Conrad Cramer, another neighbor who came in to help with the haying, declared "I have been in Mr. Rice's house many a night playing cards, and both he and Mrs. Rice were there often times looking on."[271] Cramer added that the Rices seemed to like to see people enjoying themselves.

That William Marsh Rice was enjoying the life he led in Somerset County there can be no question; among his papers is a note to the farm manager, written from New Orleans in 1882 when he and Elizabeth Baldwin Rice were on their way north after wintering in Houston. Clearly he followed every detail of what was going on at Green Brook and knew exactly how he wanted things done. "I hope you have had Mr. Trust to trim the grape vines but if he cannot then you and Cooper can manage it. Cut all of last years growth but two buds upon each limb or branch. The apple trees want the dead branches and suckers cut and pear trees ought to have half of last years growth cut and interfering limbs."[272] The fact that he made no trips to Texas at all between 1873, when the Green Brook property became wholly his, and 1878, when he and Elizabeth Baldwin Rice passed most of the winter in Houston with the Groesbeecks,[273] tells its own story. After 1877, when control of the Houston and Texas Central Railroad had passed to Charles Morgan's hands, Rice may have felt it was necessary to return to the Southwest to look into his other investments. A handwritten invitation of January 3, 1879, referring to this visit, shows that his ties to the city of Houston were far more than financial.

> The undersigned your friends feeling gratified at seeing you once more among us after your prolonged absence and understanding that it may be some time before we shall again have that pleasure, as an evidence of their personal kind feelings and of their appreciation of your active identification with the past history of our City and of every successful effort for its development would be pleased to have you join us and others of your friends in a collation to be given at the Hutchins House at some time during your visit upon one evening to be named by yourself.[274]

The signers include nearly every name associated with Houston's early history: Botts, Goldthwaite, Richardson, Baker, Stewart, Morris, Cleveland, and Groesbeeck, to name only a few. According to Emanuel Raphael, to whom William Marsh Rice was to entrust a good many of his affairs in Houston during the last years of his life, Mr. Rice confided to him at the time that he did not care for this sort of thing; he liked to see his old friends, but was averse to a public affair. One gathers that the party never came off. Mr. Rice, added Raphael, was always "a very modest man."[275]

Not long after his return to Texas, William Marsh Rice made what was to be the most valuable single investment of his life, not only in itself but for the contribution it was to make to the intellectual growth of Houston and the entire Southwest. For $1.25 an acre, he bought up nearly fifty thousand acres of government land in what is now a part of Beauregard Parish, Louisiana; land which included some of the finest standing pine anywhere in the South.[276] In this same year of 1879, William Marsh Rice II, the second of Frederick Allyn Rice's sons, received his degree in engineering from Princeton University, where his uncle William had helped to finance his studies.[277] Rice himself was sixty-three and childless; the interest in education which he had inherited from his father had been encouraged during his early years in Houston by his friendship with the Reverend Charles Gillette. The warmth of that friendship was reflected in the fact that, at the time of their marriages, Rice had sent each of Gillette's three daughters money to be used toward their trousseaux.[278] At Green Brook, William Marsh Rice would have been able to observe his nephew's progress through Princeton at firsthand, and the experience may have brought home to him how closely education was linked to wealth, particularly in those difficult post-Civil War times, and how great a handicap poverty could be to the young.

Thinking along these lines, Rice was especially drawn to the ideas of two men, Stephen Girard and Peter Cooper. Girard, the eldest in a large family in southwestern France, had cut short his schooling in order to go to work. Living near Bordeaux, he took to the sea for a trade and eventually settled in his later, wealthy years, on a country estate not far from the port of Philadelphia. Himself by then a ship owner, Girard's vessels nearly always set out with instructions to bring back "choice plants, seeds, or fruittrees."[279] In 1831 he died a childless multimillionaire and left funds in the neighborhood of six million dollars to found a school for "poor white orphan boys" which opened its doors in Philadelphia on the first of January, 1848.[280] Cooper, a sickly boy who left home in 1808 at the age of seventeen to work as a coachmaker's apprentice and who went on to amass a fortune, "often declared that he hoped no one would ever have to go through his own hard struggle to get a training."[281] After a long and careful period of planning, in 1854 he laid the cornerstone of his "workingmen's institute" in New York City.

From William Marsh Rice's Wall Street offices it was no great distance uptown to the Cooper Union on Astor Place where, well into his nineties, Peter Cooper used to stroll about observing everything that was going on. On his own testimony, Rice stopped by the Union fairly frequently,[282] and it was after a number of such visits, toward the close of 1881, that he approached John D. Bartine, a New Jersey lawyer who had handled the purchase of the Green Brook property, for the purpose of drawing up a new will.[283]

Taking Bartine with him, Rice first made a trip to Philadelphia to visit Girard College[284] and to make himself familiar with the terms of Stephen Girard's will. The ex-French cabin boy had laid down very precise guidelines for the education of orphans:

> They shall be instructed in the various branches of a sound education, comprehending reading, writing, grammar, arithmetic, geography, navigation, surveying, practical mathematics, astronomy, natural, chemical, and experimental philosophy, the French and Spanish languages . . . and such other learning and science as the capacities of the several scholars may merit or warrant; I would have them taught facts and things, rather than words or signs.[285]

Unlike Peter Cooper, who had a daughter of his own and included with his "Union of Science and Art" a school "for the instruction of respectable females in the arts of design,"[286] which constituted the first important trade-school for women in the United States, Girard limited his college to male students. In all other respects, their aims and standards ran parallel and William Marsh Rice could hardly have chosen better models for the purpose which he had in mind. Accordingly, when Bartine drew up a will for him in January, 1882, apart from annuities to his wife, his brother Frederick, his sisters Charlotte and Minerva, and his nephew Joseph Blinn, the bulk of Rice's estate was left to the governor of New Jersey and the presiding judge of the supreme court of the same state as administrators of the building and maintenance of the William M. Rice Orphans' Institute on his property in Somerset County.[287]

Always a man who believed in doing a thing thoroughly if he were going to do it at all, William Marsh Rice took considerable pains in setting out exactly what he had in mind. "Whereas I have long been deeply impressed with the importance of caring for, maintaining and educating poor children without parents to provide for, or means to educate them, and of placing them, by the early cultivation of their minds, and the development of their moral principles, above the many temptations to which, through poverty and ignorance, they are exposed . . . I am particularly desirous of providing for the maintenance and education of as many poor, male white children of American birth as possible."[288] Such "poor white fatherless male children" were to be taken into the Institute between the ages of six and ten years and to remain there no longer than their eighteenth birthday, by which time it was presumed that they would be ready to enter some trade. Preference was to be given to orphans born in Somerset County, New Jersey, and Harris County, Texas, and they were to be provided with "plain, but wholesome food, clothed with plain but decent apparel (no distinctive dress ever to be worn) and lodged in a plain but comfortable manner."[289]

Girard, who had been born in that part of France most torn in the past by religious wars, had not only forbidden any "ecclesiastic, missionary, or minister of any sect whatever" to hold any position in his college; he also refused any such person the right to visit there.[290] William Marsh Rice, for reasons which he did not divulge, made some of the same conditions, although not so absolutely. He stipulated that "all the instructors and teachers shall take pains to instill into the minds of the scholars the purest principles of morality so that on their entrance into active life they may from incliniation and habit evince benevolence towards their fellow creatures and a love of truth, sobriety and industry, and I further direct and require that no sectarianism shall be permitted in the Institution, so that the pupils may be left free to adopt such religious views as their matured reason may dictate."[291] Aside from an occasional reflection in the letters he wrote to old friends in Houston during the last years of his life, this is as near as William Marsh Rice ever came to discussing his personal philosophy; after nearly one hundred years it stands up better than most.

However successful Rice may have been at conducting his business and his philanthropies, his luck seems to have run out when it came to domestic arrangements. Elizabeth Baldwin Rice was not the sort of woman ever to be happy in the country for long; she was gregarious, she liked having friends about her and arranging for their entertainment; she found small consolation in keeping horses and a carriage when there was no one on whom to call. "Mrs. Rice got tired of living at Dunellen, [it was] lonely for her and very dull."[292] Friends spoke of visiting there and finding the house elegant, handsomely furnished, lacking in nothing; the New York decorator who supplied wallpaper and heavy lace curtains for Green Brook commented, "We always tried to cater to Mrs. Rice."[293] Eventually there was nothing left to be done in the way of furnishings and interior decoration, and the company of the Trust girls began to pall; it is surprising that Elizabeth Baldwin Rice remained in New Jersey as long as she did. William Marsh Rice used to go into New York to attend Saturday afternoon matinees with great regularity, but for some reason his wife never went with him.[294]

Rice became increasingly attached to this retreat where he had arranged to have his office overlook the chicken yard so that he could keep an eye on all that went on there,[295] and where he clearly hoped to end his days. A friend who had known Elizabeth Baldwin in San Francisco during the years of her marriage to John Brown, and who made several visits to Green Brook every year (Lilla McDougall Boothby) recalled Mr. Rice's wanting her to walk about the farm with him and inspect the recent improvements each time she came. "When do you want to finish this place?" she asked him, and was told "I hope never, while I live, because I shall always want something to amuse me."[296] Isabel Carpenter, living across the way, could understand that it might be different for a woman; it was "very lonely on [the] farm and Mrs. Rice thought she got malaria there."[297] By other accounts, it was Rice, according to his wife, who came down with malaria,[298] which would not have been too

unlikely since Green Brook was only twenty miles from central
New Jersey's Great Swamp. Laura Geddes Morton, a cousin of
Elizabeth Baldwin Rice's who later stood to gain a good deal
under her contested will and whose testimony was consistently
hostile to William Marsh Rice, said bluntly "Cousin Libbie did
not want to stay there; she hated the place."[299]

Although both Rices in the spring of 1882 spoke of being on
their way "home" as they left Houston after some weeks at the
Hutchins House and although Mrs. Rice wrote ahead that a
general housecleaning would be necessary to get things ready
for the company she was expecting from Texas,[300] by the following February William Marsh Rice had given in to her wishes
and rented an apartment at the "Grenoble," two blocks west of
Fifth Avenue on 57th Street in Manhattan.[301] If he regretted the
change, Rice never spoke of it. For several years the Rices
continued to spend a part of each summer in New Jersey and
they took pride in the fresh eggs and vegetables which were sent
up to them at the Grenoble apartment from Green Brook,[302] but
their ties to the farm gradually weakened. Elizabeth Baldwin
Rice had the best of the furniture and her favorite knick-knacks
brought in from the country place, along with Mr. Rice's cherished pictures.[303] Mrs. Morton, incidentally, thought very little
of these last, which Rice "had commissioned some friend to buy
in Europe for him." She dismissed them as "Pictures of cattle;
very large, showy pictures."[304]

At the age of fifty-six, Elizabeth Baldwin Rice must have felt
that the brilliant social life for which she had hoped was at last
within her grasp. To be sure, the Grenoble apartment was somewhat smaller than she would have liked, since it was necessary
to sacrifice the back parlor in order to have a bedroom to
herself.[305] The young wife of Charles Thornton Adams, on the
other hand, whose father-in-law Charles W. Adams had been in
partnership with William Marsh Rice at Galveston thirty years
earlier,[306] found the Rices' new home "pleasant, delightful and
roomy" and added that Mrs. Rice anticipated entertaining "on
a large scale."[307] Laura Morton's daughter, also a Laura, for her
part declared that the rooms were gloomy and not particularly

well furnished, by which she apparently meant to say "not commensurate with Rice's means."[308] The library bookshelves were not filled; there were no comfortable chairs in the parlor, and furthermore, declared Miss Morton, who clearly enjoyed every moment of giving evidence, neither at Green Brook nor at the Grenoble had she experienced the satisfaction of eating with solid silver forks.[309]

In spite of this grave social handicap, Elizabeth Baldwin Rice persevered in her campaign. The problem of keeping servants continued to give her difficulty, and one or another of the Trusts would be summoned up from New Jersey to "help out," which might mean anything from general housework and cooking to sewing for Mrs. Rice and helping her to get her trunks ready when the Rices went down to Houston. "[Mr.] Rice would not have called me a servant because I used merely to help them out at times,"[310] said Josephine, and her sister Lizzie added that Mrs. Rice very seldom gave her money. "She used to pay me in giving me different presents."[311]

Although she represented the ultimate in fashion as far as Lizzie and Josephine were concerned, Elizabeth Baldwin Rice must have felt that her move into the city was only a first step up the social ladder. The acquaintances which she made at this time speak of her frequent luncheons and afternoon receptions where all agree that she was always superbly dressed. William Marsh Rice allowed her unlimited charge accounts at a number of New York's better shops—although she complained that he would not allow her to visit any dentist other than his own in Brooklyn[312]—and her fitter at Lord and Taylor said admiringly, "I do not think any lady in New York dressed more elegantly than Mrs. Rice did."[313] She ordered a quantity of costumes every fall before her trips to Houston and often brought the store new customers from the South. In spite of the accusations later made by the Baldwin family and its partisans that William Marsh Rice was a monster of niggardliness who gave his wife so little pocket money that she was reduced to going about the city on street cars,[314] he seems on the contrary to have been genuinely proud of her good taste in dress and to have shown considerable generosity regarding her personal expenses. What he would not do was to participate in her social campaign. "Rice does not pretend to be a Chesterfield,"[315] commented Maria Van Alstyne, a friend of long standing, and even young Mrs. Adams ventured the opinion that the Rices were "very dissimilar in their tastes."[316]

The shortest route into society can be by way of an assumption of culture and the performance of good works, and of this Elizabeth Baldwin Rice was well aware. By the end of the 'eighties she was a member of the Drawing-Room Society,[317] at whose meetings one might expect readings, recitations, extemporaneous talks, plays, tableaux, and music, a Society which boasted at least one genuine literary lion in the person of William Dean Howells.[318] In 1884 she was listed among the managers of The New York Diet Kitchen Association for Providing Nourishing Food for the Sick Poor,[319] an organization that claimed without undue modesty that "the intemperate have been reclaimed, the discouraged and disappointed have been led out into the sunshine of hope . . . , the indolent or desponding have been inspired with courage and nerved to new endeavor" through its efforts.[320]

William Marsh Rice, not being a man whose interests lay among the indolent or desponding and being no longer engrossed in the care of his poultry and fruit trees, found his interest turning more and more to what was going on in Texas. Circumstances were partially responsible for this. In 1881 Rice's old friend and business associate Abraham Groesbeeck bought up the dilapidated frame building at the corner of Main and Texas Avenue, formerly known as the Capitol Hotel, which stood on the site of that improvised capitol of the Republic of Texas where President Houston had led the ladies out to dance by the light of whale-oil candles.[321] Latterly the structure had served as a boarding house. Groesbeeck undertook to demolish it, announcing that in its place he intended to put up a four-story brick hotel of about eighty rooms, with such modern conveniences as electric bells and a passenger elevator, as well as a ground floor paved in its entirety with marble.[322] As a business venture, however, the new Capitol Hotel did not live up to its promise; six months before Groesbeeck's death, the $125,000 undertaking passed into William Marsh Rice's hands at a tax sale on January 23, 1886.[323] Earlier, Rice had at least once loaned money to Groesbeeck in an effort to keep the venture afloat;[324] he was henceforth faced with the necessity of finding a manager for the hotel as well as arranging for the leases of several small shops on the street level. At about this same time, Rice was approached by the Houston Electric Light and Power Company for a loan of $3,000 in gold[325] and he took an active part in the incorporation of the Merchants and Planters Oil Company for "the manufacture and sale of cotton seed oil and oilcake, cotton seed meal and linters . . . and for the manufacture and sale of soaps."[326] All this required that he spend more and more time in Houston and, meanwhile, he was coming to the most far-reaching decision of his life.

CHAPTER III

PLANS FOR THE INSTITUTE

In 1886 the president of the Houston School Board was Cesar Maurice Lombardi, who had come to the United States from Switzerland in 1860 as a boy of fifteen and been educated at the Jesuit College in New Orleans. Settling in Houston ten years later, he was soon associated with the firm of W. D. Cleveland and Company, wholesale merchants and cotton factors, and in 1877 he married Cornelius Ennis' youngest daughter, Caroline.[327] In his old age Lombardi wrote a charming series of letters to his grandchildren, telling them something about his own life, and in the course of these he recounted the following story.

Sometime in the mid-'eighties, while travelling for his health in the western part of New York state, Lombardi noticed that "the children of the farming population in that neighborhood" were bringing home books from the nearby village of Geneseo. He subsequently learned that the Wadsworth family had assumed the maintenance of a library there which had been founded by General Wadsworth during his lifetime and he "was impressed with the amount of service that a rich man could thus confer on his community in this and other educational ways."[328] A year or so later, as president of the Houston School Board, Lombardi found he had run up against a blank wall in his petition to the City Council for funds with which to build a municipal high school. The councilmen were of the opinion, moreover, that "a High School was a highfaluting nonsense anyhow." "I was," remembered Lombardi, "in despair."[329]

Whenever he came to Houston, it was William Marsh Rice's habit to stop in fairly frequently at Lombardi's office and there to talk about old times in Texas when he and Lombardi's father-in-law had been young men making their fortunes. It was during

61

one of these visits just after the City Council's rejection of his petition, in 1886 or 1887 so far as Lombardi could recall, that he resolved to seek help in another quarter.

> I asked Mr. Rice in my private office and locked the door so we would not be disturbed. I told him of my observations at Genesee and how they suggested to me that he, Mr. Rice, might emulate old General Wadsworth and go him one better by erecting a large and well-equipped high school building in Houston, where it was so badly needed. I reminded him that he had made his fortune in Houston and that it was poetic justice that Houston should become the beneficiary of his surplus wealth. I pointed out what a monument that would be to his memory, a monument that would not crumble with time, but that would persist indefinitely in the hearts and minds of successive generations, and more to the same effect. We talked about an hour.[330]

Mr. Rice thanked him, Lombardi continued, "for calling his attention to this matter" and promised to come to some sort of decision about it before he went back to New York. Since Lombardi heard nothing more, he managed to waylay Rice on the eve of his departure and to express his disappointment at the lack of any firm commitment. He was told that Rice had recently had business reverses and consequently had not been able to come to any decision. This answer would not do at all for Lombardi's purposes, and Rice was finally driven to say that the younger man might draw up an outline of exactly what he had in mind and send it along to New York for his consideration. With this Lombardi had to be satisfied.

Lombardi's memorandum, had it survived, would have been interesting to compare with the final charter of the Rice Institute, but all that is certain is that his outline did its work. A few months later when Lombardi was himself in New York, he called on the Rices at their Grenoble apartment and "There I found him more willing, much more willing, to fall into my plans and his wife almost enthusiastic."[331] Lombardi adds that this was in the spring of the year and that there was no further communication from Rice for another twelve months or more.

> Then one evening Capt. James A. Baker, who was Mr. Rice's attorney, came to see me and told me that Mr. Rice had just arrived from New York and wished to see me next day at his room at the Hotel. . . . When, next day, I called upon him he told me that what I had told

him the year before about devoting a part of his fortune to educational purposes had made an impression upon him; that he had given the subject much thought, but that he had come to the conclusion not to erect and equip a High School building because the City as a community was under obligation to do that, that the City was able to do it, and should be made to do it. Instead, he had planned to endow an instituion of learning separate and distinct from the public school system, a sort of auxiliary to it, planned largely upon the Cooper's institute in New York and to be known at the Wm. M. Rice Institute of Literature, Science and Art; that he had frequently visited the Cooper's Institute and that the idea had grown and expanded in his mind much beyond the original conception of a mere school building, but that while he would begin right now to make provision for financing the Institution he did not wish to put his plans into effect during his life time, but only after his death.[332]

Baker's call upon Lombardi must have taken place in late April or early May, 1891. This casts some doubt on the date that Lombardi assigns to his first conversation with William Marsh Rice about the new high school, but Baker's recollection was substantiated by the statement of another man who was to be influential in guiding the future Institute, Emanuel Raphael. Raphael had been born in Birmingham, England, in 1847, but not long thereafter his father, the Reverend Samuel Raphael, brought his family to the United States and eventually to Texas, where he arrived in time to serve as Houston's rabbi during the Civil War.[333] His son had gone to work in 1863 on the new telegraph line which was being built along the Texas and New Orleans Railroad right-of-way; by 1868 he was working for the Houston and Texas Central, where he first came into contact with William Marsh Rice. By the mid-'seventies, Emanuel Raphael was the Chief Cashier of the Houston Savings Bank and as such participated in a number of Rice's business transactions; by 1880 he had gone on to become the president of the Houston Electric Light and Power Company.[334]

By May, 1891, Raphael was serving as a trustee of the Houston public school system and he called upon Rice at the Capitol Hotel in the hope of interesting a man whom he knew to be both wealthy and childless in the future of the city's schools; specifically, he asked Rice to give some support to a library fund drive. Rice countered with the same statement that he had made to

Lombardi, namely, that the city could and should assume the responsibility for its own public education system. He then revealed his own plan for the endowment of an "Institute and polytechnic school" to be situated in Houston and asked Raphael if he would consent to serve as one of the trustees.[335]

Very rarely during his lifetime did Rice's judgment of human nature turn out to have been mistaken, although in his last years he grudgingly admitted to having guessed wrong once or twice. In the case of Emanuel Raphael he could hardly have made a better choice for what he had in mind. Together they drew up an instrument incorporating Rice's ideas for his Institute and Raphael then went around to see the other men whom Rice had selected as trustees, in order to make the offer known to them. In addition to Rice himself, Raphael and Lombardi, they included Rice's brother Frederick; James Baker, his attorney; Alfred S. Richardson, who like Rice was a director of the Houston and Texas Central Railway and a vestryman of Christ Church; and James E. McAshan, a young banker and native-born Texan. All accepted.[336]

Under a deed of indenture dated May 13, 1891, the trustees agreed to hold Rice's note for $200,000, together with the "interest, issue, income and profits thereof" as an endowment "devoted to the instruction and improvement of the white inhabitants of the City of Houston and State of Texas, through and by the establishment and maintenance of a Public Library and Institute for the Advancement of Literature, Science and Art."[337] It is reasonable to assume that all of the documents covering the establishment and incorporation of the Institute were drawn up with the advice of Baker, as an attorney, as well as that of the two others who had already spoken out so strongly in the cause of education, Raphael and Lombardi, but now and again the founder's voice comes through quite distinctly, as in the article which stipulates that "should there at any time be a difference of opinion, between the party of the first part [i.e., Rice] and said Trustees as to the investment or expenditure of said funds, or the management of said Institute, then the decision of the said party of the first part shall control."[338]

On May 19, 1891, the charter of the William M. Rice Institute was incorporated in Austin. The heart of Rice's intent was expressed in two paragraphs in the indenture agreement that echo the thought of Cooper and Girard as well as those that had led to the founding of Rice's now superseded Orphans' Institute at Green Brook. The Endowment Fund, this agreement stated, was to provide "for the establishment and maintenance of a thorough polytechnic school, for males and females, designed to give instructions on the application of Science and Art to the useful occupations of life" and it was further specified that the "Library, Reading Room, Scientific Departments and Polytechnic School and the instruction, benefits and enjoyment to be derived from the Institute [were] to be free."[339]

As Raphael himself indicated, William Marsh Rice was a very private man. "Being quite an old man and a strict businessman, Rice had his peculiarities with relation to dealing and doing business with people."[340] The fact that he wanted no publicity in connection with this princely gift he was making to the city of Houston undoubtedly sprang less from his peculiarities, however, than from the wish to protect himself from the onslaught of begging letters which inevitably pursue any man known to possess great wealth. The same instinct was probably responsible for the image of himself which Rice allowed to circulate in his old age, that of a grasping octogenarian whose only interest was money; there is evidence to suggest that he was occasionally amused by the thought of proving the public to have been wrong. For all his years in Texas, there was a great deal of New England in Rice's character to the very end.

The estate at Green Brook had been sold the previous February[341] "for a song," as Emanuel Raphael very accurately observed[342] in view of the fact that the buyer paid the Rices only $10,000 for the four tracts of land "with all houses, buildings, trees, ways, waters, profits, privileges and advantages."[343] Why Rice agreed to take such a loss on the place was another of the decisions which he kept to himself, and one of the few times when he is known to have taken a financial loss. The only roughly comparable instance occurred during the depression of

1893, with the failure of the City Bank of Houston, of which Rice was one of the largest depositors.[344]

Sometime between the sale of the Green Brook property and the incorporation of the William M. Rice Institute, Elizabeth Baldwin Rice decided that the apartment at the Grenoble would not do; not only was her bed-sitting room arrangement an inconvenience, but the rooms taken all together were too small for her to entertain properly.[345] Accordingly, when the Rices returned to New York in the summer of 1891, it was to another, larger apartment in the same building, where Mrs. Rice declared herself to be much happier.[346] There, at the end of January, 1892, Elizabeth Baldwin Rice drew up a will leaving the income from her estate to her husband if he survived her, and, after his death, divided that estate among an assortment of cousins, nephews, nieces, a brother, sister, and people whom she currently looked upon as her friends, as well as three Houston churches, the "Bayland Orphan Home" of Harris County, and the Woman's Exchange, the Diet Kitchen, and the Society for the Prevention of Cruelty to Animals and Children in New York City and, somewhat surprisingly, "The C. M. Allen Institute of Houston, Texas."[347]

Charlotte Allen was, of course, Elizabeth Baldwin Rice's aunt and the first of the Baldwin clan to come out to Texas; she lived on until 1906 and in 1892 was still one of the great ladies of Houston society. Whether this represents a last-ditch attempt to keep the Baldwins, as it were, on the map, or whether Mrs. Rice had forgotten that her husband had elected to give his own name to his Institute, is hard to say. Like most people, she was probably more complicated than she gave the impression of being, and to dismiss her as spoiled, vain, and empty-headed may be unfair. In an age when women were brought up to do little more than look after a home and children, she was childless, gregarious, and not very resourceful. Emanuel Raphael recalled that in later years she frequently talked with him about the Institute, urging him to use his influence with Mr. Rice and press for a beginning on the construction itself.[348] She fancied herself emerging as a patroness of the fine arts and spoke of having a marble bust made of William Marsh Rice which would be set in the main entrance to the Institute, as well as of the park which she envisioned encircling the buildings, set out with trees and flowering shrubs.[349] Mr. Rice had promised her, she told Raphael, that if there should be a vacancy on the board of trustees she would be appointed to fill it.

William Marsh Rice himself confirmed this to Raphael.[350] He also, in deference to his wife's eagerness to be associated with the new undertaking, arranged that she should be a cosigner with him of the four deeds of gift which Raphael drew up when the Rices were in Houston again the following June. By the first of these deeds, the William M. Rice Institute was deeded nearly ten thousand acres in Jones County, Texas; by the second, a voluminous document on which James Baker as well as Raphael worked for nearly a month, the timber holdings in Louisiana which Rice had bought from the government were made a part of the endowment fund. Rice had also been giving thought in the interval since he was last in Houston to the location of his new Institute and had settled on a tract of nearly seven acres which he owned fronting on Louisiana Street. Known as the Ennis tract, it had been pledged to Rice by Cornelius Ennis as security for a loan; Ennis being unable to repay on schedule, Rice had taken up the property, a proceeding which caused no hard feelings on Ennis' part, according to one of his descendants.[351] The veteran Houstonian evidently knew his man.

The third deed was accordingly listed as "Site of the Institute" and the fourth and last made a gift to the endowment fund of the Capitol Hotel property, although its revenues were to go to the Rices during their lifetime. Raphael remembered all the details of the transaction. He brought the deeds himself around to the Rices' rooms at the Capitol at about eight o'clock in the evening; James Baker was present and a notary public named Bocock. Before Elizabeth Baldwin Rice signed anything, her husband left the room and Bocock explained to her in some detail exactly what it was that she was fixing her signature to. According to Raphael she was enthusiastic over the idea of being a participant in Mr. Rice's undertaking and "smiled pleasantly all the time."[352] Raphael, knowing William Marsh Rice's dislike of publicity, on his own initiative told Bocock not to enter the deeds upon the notarial records; only in the September following, when the city council proposed to drive streets through the Louisiana Street property, did he advise Rice to have that particular gift put on record so that the land could be preserved intact.[353] This registration duly took place, but with so little fanfare that the general public of Houston remained unaware of the plans that were being made for its future.

His Institute was thus becoming more and more of a source of satisfaction to him, but, on the other hand, William Marsh Rice's hotel was not. His difficulties in maintaining the Capitol may even have been partly responsible for his determination not to see a single stone set in place for the Institute buildings during his life time. Elizabeth Baldwin Rice told James McAshan that her husband had declared the responsibility for such an undertaking would positively shorten his life[354] and to a Houston acquaintance who called on him in New York shortly thereafter Rice remarked "somewhat testily," "I think I should know what is the best thing to do to secure my own happiness. It would be no pleasure to me to have these buildings constructed."[355] Something was always needing attention at the Capitol Hotel: furniture wore out and had to be replaced; shop leases had to be renewed; each year the cost of heating the building through the winter months became dearer and dearer, and McGinly, the manager, gave him nothing but hard-luck stories and bigger bills to pay. The final outrage, in Rice's eyes, were the exorbitant charges which were presented to him each year during his winter stay at the hotel, in rooms which were none too comfortable and where Mrs. Rice found it difficult to entertain her friends as she would have liked to.[356] And how the bills for punch, coffee, lemonade, "bisquit Glase," and Mr. Rice's Apollinaris water did mount up![357]

Rice's solution was prompt and characteristic. For years an old rat-infested stable had been left standing behind the Capitol; since one of McGinly's complaints was a lack of sufficient accommodations, the stable would be pulled down and an annex to the hotel put up in its place in which the Rices would have their own private apartments.[358] By the following year, 1893, the Annex was under way and William Marsh Rice took Raphael around to the building site to point out the excellent brick he was using and to describe his own quarters, which were to overlook Texas Avenue and to include a large office for himself as well as reception rooms for Mrs. Rice, the whole to be finished off "in fine woods."[359] When they were not in Houston, their apartment was to be closed off and kept in readiness for them at all times[360]

Rice was not, however, the only one to think of enlarging his accommodations; at almost the same time the manager of the Grenoble apartments began work on an addition to the building which threatened, both Rices felt, to block out their light and air.[361] Although their lease had nearly a year still to run, friends who called on them in the late summer of 1894 found that the disorder of moving was already apparent: rugs were up, pictures down, and packing cases stood about in the hallways.[362] To Alice Adams, who lunched with her in the early autumn, Elizabeth Baldwin Rice declared that when they returned from Texas the following spring, she and Mr. Rice intended to move into a much larger apartment on Madison Avenue, where it would be possible to entertain on a more generous scale.[363] One problem was ingeniously solved when William Marsh Rice remarked to John Matheson, a cabinetmaker who had done a number of jobs for him at the Grenoble, that Mrs. Rice was tired of what she called "the old style furniture." Matheson suggested that they send the old pieces down to Houston to furnish the apartment then being built in the Annex and begin all over again in New York with something more in fashion.[364] This practicality must have pleased Rice; he saw to it that the chairs were "fresh upholstered" before they went out to Texas and he himself went around to a number of furniture auctions where he picked up a pair of black walnut bookcases and several walnut wardrobes, which were also shipped to the Capitol.[365] A visiting friend from Houston remembered that Rice said cheerfully to his wife, as they were discussing the new Madison Avenue flat, "My lady, I would like you to be here and select new furniture for this apartment when I take it."[366]

By the following spring, their suite in the Capitol Annex was ready for them, down to Mr. Rice's cherished pictures, which had been sent to Houston so that they might one day hang in his Institute. Elizabeth Baldwin Rice must have felt that socially she had arrived; in New York, her name and her husband's had appeared for the first time that year in the pages of the *Social Register* and hers, although not Mr. Rice's, was soon to be listed in the *Society List and Club Register.*[367] In Houston itself, the outstanding social event of the season took place in May, when the United Confederate Veterans gathered for their thirtieth reunion. Jefferson Davis' youngest child, Winnie, "The Daughter of the Confederacy," honored Houston with her presence and Mrs. Rice's reception for Miss Davis was the talk of the town for days. The reporter for the Galveston *Daily News,* although dazzled, was certainly at no loss for words.

> The reception given by Mrs. William M. Rice in her suite of elegant rooms in the Capitol Hotel today from 11 to 1 o'clock was one of the elegant social functions of the reunion. Perhaps 500 invitations had been sent, hence the elite and fashion of the occasion was there. The rooms had been tastefully arranged and a string band furnished gentle music in accord with the low and melodious hum of feminine voices and the ripple of sweetest laughter . . . .The beauty and loveliness of not only Houston but all the southland were there in divine perfection.[368]

The "beautiful gray satin" which Elizabeth Baldwin Rice wore on this occasion—for all the ladies were turned out in "full dress," which must have been something of a trial in Houston in late May—had been ordered at Lord and Taylor especially for Miss Davis' visit,[369] as had the "gold parlor chairs" and "little fur rugs" which the discriminating Laura Baldwin Morton had admired in her cousin's New York apartment the previous autumn.[370] "Mrs. Rice said she would rather live in Houston, because when she was in New York, she was one of many, and when she was in Houston, to use a slang expression, she could be very swell," testified a friend who had long known the Rices both in the South and the North,[371] but another acquaintance insisted on the contrary. "Mrs. Rice told me she preferred New York. She loved New York. She loved the life of New York. She told me she could go here [and there] and have diversions, just as she pleased, and she could not get them in Houston."[372]

The truth of the matter may well have been that Elizabeth Baldwin Rice was an insecure woman seeking reassurance as to her own importance. There is also evidence to suggest that she had for a time been unwell; two ladies who called on her just before the Confederate Reunion mention that she received them resting on a couch in the small parlor.[373] Laura Baldwin Morton, on the contrary, maintained that when the Rices returned to New York that year her cousin was "in better health and cleverer in conversation than she had been during the time of her illness when she had had [an] attack of pneumonia."[374] Miss Morton had reason to insist on Mrs. Rice's soundness of mind, for she soon stood to gain some $25,000 by it. The following spring saw a train of events put into motion which led straight into the United States law courts and came very close to costing William Marsh Rice, and Houston, their Institute.

Elizabeth Baldwin Rice's health took a turn for the worse during the winter of 1895, after the Rices had returned to what both of them apparently considered only a "temporary" apartment in the Hoffman Arms, at 640 Madison Avenue.[375] In late April, 1896, Rice brought her back to Houston in the hope that warm weather would make her more comfortable, but shortly thereafter she suffered what can only have been a fairly severe stroke.

Mrs. Rice rode out the last time 13 of May. One [sic] the morning of 14th she said she was not well but did not wish to put her self in the hands of a physitian [sic] as she could not tell when she should get out. Dr. Rutherford came the next day likely by action of Mrs. Huntington.

Rutherford said he could relieve her in about a week or ten days at furtherest so she would be able to travel and advised her going to Ashville North Carolina proposing to take her there. The heat was very oppressive. The Dr. continued to visit her twice a day and always saying in a short time she would be able to travel. She did not improve but her condition became more confirmed.

She was taken sick in the room adjoining my office but soon moved into a cooler room in the annex building fronting on Travis St. Mrs. Huntington & Mrs. Holt took charge of her. Trained nurses attended upon her. One white & two colored & Mrs. Rice's maid Clara Schaffner.

Her right side—leg and arm—was paralyzed so that she had no use of them. Her speech was so much affected that I could with great difficulty understand her at any time and some times could not make out her wants. Her mind was much impaired.

She gradually grew worse, the weather was very warm which operated greatly against her. She grew weaker in all respects . . . .Her mind was much enfeebled and she was not herself at all. Totally incapable of doing any business.[376]

So William Marsh Rice was convinced. Nevertheless, on the first of June, 1896, Elizabeth Baldwin Rice signed a lengthy new will about which her husband knew nothing. It was drawn up for her by a lawyer named Orren Thaddeus Holt,[377] who, with his wife, had that spring taken rooms at the Capitol Hotel very near the Rices.[378] Orren Holt had first had dealings with William Marsh Rice some years earlier, when Holt was hired by the Houston and Texas Central to settle claims made against it by ranchers whose cattle had been killed when they strayed onto the unfenced tracks.[379] During the early summer of 1896 his wife quickly became one of those intimate friends whom Elizabeth Baldwin Rice was given to making on short notice, and it was Mrs. Holt, together with Mamie Huntington, a Baldwin niece from Cleveland, who remained continually with Mrs. Rice after she was taken ill.[380]

Under the directions of the new will, which was witnessed by Mrs. Holt's mother and sister, Holt was to be Mrs. Rice's executor; for this service he was to receive ten percent of "all amounts received and paid out by him under the terms of this will."[381] At the very least, this would have assured to him something in the nature of $120,000, for in the opening phrases of her extraordinary testament Elizabeth Baldwin Rice described herself as a resident of the County of Harris and the State of Texas and thereby under the Texas law of community property was empowered to dispose of one-half of all assets acquired by her husband in the course of their marriage.[382] Even more significantly, although she directed that $250,000 be set aside to endow a home for indigent gentlewomen in Baldwinsville, New York, which was to be known as the "Elizabeth Baldwin Home" and that another $100,000 be allotted to set up the Elizabeth Baldwin Park in Houston, the "Wm. M. Rice Library Building" was to receive only $15,000 and that was designated specifically to cover the purchase of portraits of "my beloved husband William M. Rice and my aunt, Charlotte Allen" and to hang those portraits therein. Of Mr. Rice's Institute there was no mention.

There were other revelations yet to come. Toward the close of Mrs. Rice's new will there was a paragraph which began, "I do solemnly declare that if I signed any papers at any time, giving away or willing away any of my property, I did so without knowing their purpose and so declare them void."[383] An exception was made in the case of the "Louisiana lands," but Mrs. Rice firmly repudiated any other such documents, maintaining that they "were not read to me," and the passage concluded with the sentence "And I trust my husband William M. Rice will give no trouble to my executor in regard to my Will, as I have considered this writing of my will for many months."[384]

All in ignorance of this thunderbolt, Rice had taken steps to act upon Dr. Rutherford's suggestion that Mrs. Rice be moved away from the oppressive heat of Houston; he settled on the Park Hotel at Waukesha in Wisconsin, which enjoyed no small reputation as a restorative watering place for invalids of all kinds. Together with Mrs. Rice travelled Rutherford, her nurse, Bessie Campbell, and a young man named Alex Stanberry who had been working for Rice in Houston for some time as a clerk, "a good, kind man and strong to lift [Mrs. Rice]."[385]

"After we left Houston and got in a cooler more bracing atmosphere, she improved, and had more energy," recalled William Marsh Rice.[386] It is difficult to believe that any permanent recovery could have been expected, however, although Rice spoke of taking his wife to New York as soon as the weather improved.[387] He remained at Waukesha himself for about three weeks and then went on to New York "for his health and at the doctor's orders."[388] "I was not well there and had to come where I could have the convenience of a home to keep myself well. She understood this and wished it," he wrote to Mrs. Morton later on in the summer.[389] By that time, however, Elizabeth Baldwin Rice had already suffered a second stroke and after a third, some three weeks after Rice's departure, she died at nine in the morning of July 24.[390]

Alex Stanberry was the only remaining member of the party which had travelled from Houston to Waukesha with Mrs. Rice, for she had taken an invalid's arbitrary dislike to Dr. Rutherford and Bessie Campbell and their stay at the Park Hotel was a short one.[391] Acting on William Marsh Rice's instructions, Stanberry sent all of Mrs. Rice's personal effects back to Texas and proceeded to New York himself to take over the job of looking after Rice. The latter's health was by then "very good" but he had decided "to always have [Mr. Stanberry] or some other to wait upon me, and take care of me where ever I am as I am too old to go about by myself."[392] Rice had returned not to the Hoffman Arms but to a flat in the Berkshire Apartments at 500 Madison Avenue which he and Elizabeth Baldwin Rice had arranged the previous winter to rent from yet another Baldwin cousin, Mary Turnure.[393] He was there, with Stanberry in attendance, when his Houston lawyers in late September sent him the astonishing news that Orren Holt had filed for probate in Texas a will whose existence William Marsh Rice had not even suspected, apparently drawn by Elizabeth Baldwin Rice.

James Baker gave it as his opinion that Mr. Rice should return to Houston immediately in order to contest this will on the grounds that Mrs. Rice was not mentally capable of knowing what she was doing at the time of its writing.[394] It is hard not to agree that Baker's inference was a correct one and there are details which suggest that there may have been some sort of collusion among those around Elizabeth Baldwin Rice after she was first stricken. Her niece, Mamie Huntington, and Orren

Holt's wife reportedly never left her side, and it was Mrs. Huntington who retained the services of Dr. Rutherford and of Bessie Campbell, the nurse. Under the terms of the will of June 1, 1896, the former would receive $25,000 and the latter $5,000[395] and it could not have been to the advantage of either to testify that their patient had not been in her right mind. Holt's enormous fee as executor—and the will stipulated that all of Elizabeth Baldwin Rice's bequests should be doubled in the event that her husband's estate turned out to be larger than she knew—was only one suggestive item; Mrs. Huntington, who had never even been mentioned in any earlier will of her aunt's, was left $200,000 outright; her daugher, Lillian, was to receive $100,000, and Jonas Baldwin, her father, $50,000 for his use during his lifetime which was to pass to Mrs. Huntington on his death.

William Marsh Rice left the following account among his papers. "About four days before we left Houston I laid down on the bed beside Mrs. Rice. She seemed to be a little brighter than usual. She said I ought to be under obligation to her for something she had not done. She said she had been greatly urged by others. I supposed she alluded to a will but in her feeble condition I asked no questions. I told her I appreciated her consideration of me."[396]

His testimony and the internal evidence notwithstanding, Mrs. Rice's will was admitted to probate by the County Court of Harris County in March, 1897.[397] It has been suggested that the climate of opinion in Houston favored its admission, since in addition to establishing the Elizabeth Baldwin Park in that city, Mrs. Rice had made generous bequests to the Parish Aid Society of Christ Church, the First Presbyterian Church, the Faith Home of Houston, and the Bayland Orphanage; perhaps these bequests had something to do with the speedy admission of her will to probate.[398] Upon the advice of his counsel, William Marsh Rice then filed suit against Holt in the U. S. Circuit Court for the Eastern District of Texas, sitting at Galveston, in which he claimed to be, and always since his second marriage to have been, a resident of the state of New York. As such, his property was not subject to disposal by his wife under the laws of Texas, and he prayed the court to remove the cloud on his title to his real property in that state.[399] For a quiet man who shunned the limelight, all this public skirmishing must have been unwelcome. What Rice mercifully could not know was that his action against Holt was only the first in a series of events that would end in newspaper headlines across the country and involve him in a melodrama more spectacular than anything he had witnessed in all his Saturday afternoons at the theater.

In September, 1896, at about the time when William Marsh Rice, at Baker's urging, was on his way to Houston from New York, a trunk arrived in Galveston from Waukesha. It had been sent by Alex Stanberry, who packed up some of his own belongings at the same time that he was getting Mrs. Rice's together, to a young friend named Charles Freeman Jones; the two men had met a year or so earlier when both were working in Galveston at the Star Flour Mill.[400] According to Jones, Stanberry had written him that the trunk was on its way and that Jones was to keep it in his room until Stanberry came to pick it up. Shortly afterward, Jones maintained, he received an anonymous letter suggesting that there was something suspect about the trunk and that he had better turn it over to Mr. Rice. Jones first wrote Stanberry, who disclaimed any knowledge of either letter or trunk, and then consulted the Galveston police chief. In the latter's presence the trunk was opened and found to contain "a great deal of Mrs. Rice's wearing apparel, such stuff as dresses, shoes, clothes," laces, and so forth.[401]

"On the same afternoon," continued Jones, "I took a train to Houston and went to Mr. Rice's office. I had never seen Mr. Rice before." The younger man told his story "just as plainly as I could," after which Rice thanked him and asked to be informed if there were any further developments. As he was leaving the Capitol Hotel, Jones was stopped by Stanberry, who had accompanied Mr. Rice back to Texas, and asked whether he needed work. Jones admitted that he did, having quit his job at the flour mill some months before, and the following afternoon he was taken on at the Capitol as a storekeeper at a salary of $20 a month and his board.[402]

In 1896 Charles Jones, or Charlie as nearly everybody called him, was twenty-one years old. The son of a tenant farmer in Harris County, he received very little formal education and along in his late teens went to work for an older brother on a schooner that carried freight between Galveston and Lynchburg, Texas. He seems to have had a knack of making himself agreeable and of getting along with people wherever he was, and at the time of William Marsh Rice's death, four years later, was described as "a tall, well-set-up young fellow with clean-cut features, a soft, well-modulated voice, and gentle, unobtrusive manners."[403]

It would have been easy for Rice to see in Jones' career a great many similarities to his own. Whether or not Alex Stanberry was able to give a satisfactory explanation of how the trunk containing Mrs. Rice's clothes had turned up in Galveston, Rice lost confidence in him; two years later he was still sufficiently irritated to refer to Stanberry as "a big rascal."[404] Rice remained on in Houston as usual through the winter after his wife's death; he had half-a-dozen major business enterprises to attend to and the usual maintenance problems at the Capitol Hotel, and he was troubled over the issue of Elizabeth Baldwin Rice's will. After this last was admitted to probate and his attorneys had determined to carry their appeal to the Federal Courts, it became apparent that the case would be a prolonged one and Rice therefore determined to return to New York in the spring of 1897. As he had observed to Laura Morton, he needed some sort of manservant, and, according to Charlie Jones' subsequent testimony, around mid-April Jones was summoned into Mr. Rice's office and offered the job of secretary and general factotum, which he accepted. Rice and Jones left Houston on May 7 and arrived in New York three days later;[405] although he did not know it, William Marsh Rice had said his goodbyes in Texas for the last time.

Some idea of Jones' duties can be gathered from a letter which Rice wrote to his business agent in Houston about a year later, when the young Texan seems to have had a brief siege of homesickness and decided that he wanted to go back to his father's farm and become a fruit-grower; seeking a replacement, Rice put down some of his requirements. "I want a nice honest young man who is not afraid to do anything. He will be the only man or person I will have. So he will have to do all there is to be done. Be Chamber Maid Cook and sort of Secretary. He will have to cook for himself and me and when the food is on the table will sit to the table and take his meals with me . . . .I prefer to have a mild unpretentious young man whose parents are plain honest religious people."[406]

"When I first went with Mr. Rice I got $25 a month and my board. This was until January first, 1898. He then raised my salary to $50 a month and all expenses. I worked for that salary until January first, 1900, when he gave me $100 a month and I paid my own expenses."[407] Jones did not explain why he changed his mind about leaving New York, but nothing more appears to have been said about the fruit farm. In the meantime, William Marsh Rice and his manservant remained in the apartment which had been originally engaged at 500 Madison Avenue until November, 1897, and then moved into another suite of rooms on the fifth floor of the same building, where they were to remain until Rice's death.

Rice had three more years yet to live, and although these were to end in tragedy, the interval was a fairly happy one. Rice settled into a self-centered bachelorhood, going out very little, absorbed in the ups and downs of his own digestion and the other aspects of his health, well looked after by his young man Charlie Jones. Jones opened the mail, ran Mr. Rice's errands and did his shopping, and lent a hand when it was necessary with the meals which the old gentleman sometimes liked to cook up for himself over a gas ring.[408] Rice subscribed to a number of periodicals with such titles as "Hygiene: Herald of Health"[409] and fussed a good deal over his diet, a remarkably sensible one consisting mainly of fresh eggs and vegetables, whole-grain bread, milk,[410] and a packaged food marketed under the name of "Granula" which appears to have been a sort of coarse-ground breakfast cereal that he constantly urged on his friends and acquaintances.[411] He was always on the look-out for new aids to his digestion and preferred whenever it was possible to diagnose, and to prescribe for, his own ailments. "I have hardly had a Doctor in my life unless for severe injoury [sic]," he observed to Charlotte Rice McKee in the spring of 1899. "Mrs. Rice used to be running after a Doctor it cost a pile of money but my expense has been but trifling."[412]

William Marsh Rice's last years were in no way characterized by a mental decline; on the contrary, his mind remained as sharp as ever and his business correspondence from this period is astonishing, both in its volume and its grasp of detail. The great bulk of these letters in the last decade of his life are addressed to the man whom he was fortunate enough to have looking after his interests in Houston and whom one suspects Rice did not appreciate as much as he ought to have. At about the time the two men were putting together their ideas for the Rice Institute, Rice had asked Emanuel Raphael to find him an enterprising and trustworthy young man who could safely be put in charge of all his business affairs in Texas. Raphael promptly summoned his twenty-two-year-old brother-in-law, Arthur B. Cohn, down from Little Rock, and Cohn began working for Rice in June, 1893.[413] From the first he exhibited a scrupulous integrity and a dedication to his work that ought to have satisfied the most demanding employer; nonetheless, William Marsh Rice never lost an opportuntiy over the years to lecture Cohn on business tactics as well as on employee relations. "Money is a very delicate property to handle when not the property of the party who is handling it," he observed on one occasion. "I do not apprehend any trouble in this case but think it best to settle this point for future operations."[414]

Arthur Cohn, who seems to have been one of the few people not overawed by Rice's wealth and reputation, replied briskly in kind from time to time. "In the repairing of the Annex you may be sure I will not be swindled by any of them. All the people with whom I deal know that I am not to be swindled. I always get my work done before I pay for it, then I'm sure to

be on the right side."[415] What is remarkable throughout these
scores of exchanges—for William Marsh Rice frequently draft-
ed his answers on the back of Cohn's original communication—
is Rice's extraordinary clarity of mind and his capacity for
storing up detail. During the repairs made to the Capitol Hotel
after a fire in the spring of 1899, he emerged from his seclusion
and went around New York, at the age of 83, inspecting the
different brands of fire hose that were available and could be
counted on to prevent a repetition of the damage; discussing the
various merits of these, he also reminds Cohn that in the past
"there was a tin worker over on the Bayou" who had done good
work for him at a fair price.[416] The February following he sent
Cohn explicit instructions on how the hotel's new carpeting was
to be laid down: over a doubled layer of paper lining, as that
would be sure to result in longer wear.[417] From the letters to
Cohn emerge anecdotes from William Marsh Rice's past inter-
spersed with sudden nuggets of business advice: complaining of
the money which had been spent improving property around
Waco in the winter of 1898, he observed that the town itself was
"an awful dull place. At one time it was lively about the time
the Railroads were striking it" and then adds without a break
"It is best to say little and think much."[418]

There was nothing with which Cohn was not expected to deal.
On one occasion Rice complained because the Houston *Post*
sometimes took as long as four days to reach him and cost more
in New York than it did in Texas into the bargain.[419] In the next
letter, Rice might ask why the Golden Crown cigars which he
ordered directly from Havana remained in stock at the Capitol's
tobacco shop for so long.[420] Categorically he asked not to be
forwarded any begging letters "unless in some female hand,"[421]
and then, for reasons which he kept to himself, was as generous
toward the writers of some of these last as he was abrupt in
refusing help to others: Mary Louise Bremond, the former Vicomtesse de Valernes who became Paul Bremond's third wife
and thus after a fashion William Marsh Rice's stepmother-in-
law, was turned down without hesitation,[422] but to Kate Van
Alstyne, another distant Bremond connection, he sent $100 or

more annually for a number of years.[423] When Cohn was not inquiring why the "Turkish Bath Rooms" at the Capitol so consistently lost money,[424] he could address himself to the problem of Emma Warren, who seems to have tried everyone's patience. Mrs. Warren, who presumably was one of Elizabeth Baldwin Rice's former servants, presented herself weekly at Cohn's office during the winter months to collect the dollar which Rice had directed should be paid to her. This outflow of cash troubled Rice and he instructed Arthur Cohn to make her an alternate offer, which was promptly refused. "I have stopped paying Emma Warren $1.00 per week as per your directions and have offered to let her have one of the Sabine Street houses, but she will not take it. Says she earns her rent where she is by milking cows and the people around her help her to get work and she is afraid she cannot make a living for herself and family if she moves into a strange neighborhood."[425]

Five years after he went to work for Rice, Cohn felt it was time to ask for a raise. It was promptly refused. Neither his original letter, nor William Marsh Rice's answer, has turned up among the Rice papers, but there is a copy of Cohn's subsequent reply pointing out that the volume of his duties remained constant, whatever the shape that business was in, and that if Mr. Rice did not feel his services were worth $150 a month there were doubtless others who did.[426] Rice must have had an inkling that Arthur Cohn was well-nigh irreplaceable, for the subject never came up again and Cohn continued to attend to the affairs of the Houston Ice and Brewing Company, the Houston Brick Works, the Texas Star Soap Company, and the other businesses in which Rice was involved, as well as the Rice Ranch, which lay to the southwest of the city of Houston and gave almost as much trouble as the Capitol Hotel.

A very different collection of letters dates from this period of William Marsh Rice's life, one that gives a glimpse of his old-fashioned gallantry when it came to the ladies. Even the sharp-tongued Laura Baldwin Morton had been obliged to confess his many kindnesses to her: buggy rides when she was a child visiting at Green Brook; small, thoughtful gifts as she grew older.[427] Now in his eighties, Rice kept in touch with one or two old Houston acquaintances, widows with whom he could exchange reminiscences that dated from the early days of the Republic. One of these, Maria Van Alstyne, had like himself moved to New York and was later to describe how in July, 1899, Rice had made one of his infrequent sorties from the Berkshire to call on her, because he had heard that her daughter's home in Houston was being sold for taxes.[428]

His most regular correspondent was Mary Andrus Brewster, a New York girl who had come out to Texas in 1844 and not long thereafter married Robert Brewster in Christ Church at about the same period that the Reverend Mr. Gillette officiated at the marriage of Julia Elizabeth Baldwin to her first husband, John H. Brown.[429] Rice was not the only gentleman to respond to Mary Brewster's charm; "General Magruder . . . , so neat, so elegant, so fond of ladies' company, was fortunate in claiming the friendship of this noble woman . . . .On that fateful occasion when he set out to recapture Galveston he bowed low over her hand and said, 'Madam, I believe that "the prayer of the righteous availeth much", and I beg of you your prayers now'."[430]

William Marsh Rice, while he may not have been as elegant, was certainly neat, and unquestionably shared the general's admiration for Mrs. Brewster. Among his papers are a number of letters written to her after he became a widower and a scattering of hers to him. While the subject of his health, and hers, takes up a certain amount of space, it gave him evident pleasure to speak of mutual acquaintances and to elaborate on his philosophy of life. "I lead a very quiet life—go out when I wish—taking my man with me. I can look out of my back windows on to the Fifth Avenue and see the passing. The cathedral is in sight at about half a block, and the music of the chimes is very pleasant [sic]. I do not worry—attend to my business and read when not otherwise engaged—and am contented, probably more here than I would be anywhere else."[431] He sent her a number of magazines, including *The Century* and the *Home Journal*, asking to be reminded when these subscriptions expired, and she wrote in return that on Wednesdays and Saturdays friends joined her in reading the *Home Journal* aloud so that at those times "you will know I am talking about my dear old friend William."[432]

More than once Rice speaks of the satisfaction which Mary Brewster's son and his family must have brought to her, adding regretfully that he himself had "no such consolation and comfort."[433] He has something to say in nearly every letter about her garden, over which she appears to have taken great pains, sometimes sending him a bunch of her early violets. "I remember your big parlor which is so large and comfortable of an afternoon, and the fruit & flowers, freshly picked."[434] He wrote Mrs. Brewster of how Cornelius Ennis' death had grieved him, as did the loss of those young men who had volunteered in 1898 to fight against Spain only to die in camp of yellow fever. Rice had few illusions about war and none whatsoever about glory, but the men to whom he might have spoken about these things were all gone. "I remember the last time I saw Old Sam [Houston]. I think it was in 1863 the year he died. He had been making a speech and came in to my store and bought a few shoes for his children and said good by. Things looked very blue and he seemed depressed. I remember him as he stood and turned to the door going out."[435]

To Mary Brewster, Rice occasionally revealed that sense of humor which would have come as a surprise to many. "Once in August I came out from New York when the fever was raging in New Orleans. I think the 23d day of the month, three hundred dying on that day. I was quarantined at Galveston but got on to a cattle steamer . . . [and] after we got up to the Bayou got on boared a Houston steamer. Got off early in [the] morning and went home. Was arrested and taken before the Mayor Col Nathan Fuller whom you well knew. The Col said he guess[ed] he would let me off as he did not think there was any danger of contagion from me laughing. He was a very pleasent man."[436]

CHAPTER IV

"MURDER ON MADISON AVENUE"

In the summer of 1898, Rice apologized to Mary Andrus Brewster for not writing more regularly, adding that he did not always feel cheerful enough to do so because of his continuing troubles over "the big suit."[437] That suit, of course, was his appeal against the validity of Elizabeth Baldwin Rice's will, still making its snail-like way into court. Mrs. Rice's executor, Orren Holt, preparing to defend his claims in Texas, found that he could not take evidence both there and in New York at the same time and late in 1898 he engaged the services of a lawyer then residing in New York City named Albert T. Patrick, to represent him in "the taking of testimony and the interviewing of witnesses." For these services, Patrick was to receive a fee of $500 plus an additional payment of $10,000 out of any sums which might be recovered from "the said William M. Rice."[438] The last of the important figures in Rice's story had made his appearance.

Albert T. Patrick had been born in Grimes County, Texas, on February 20, 1866. His parents later moved to Austin, where his father was freight agent for the Houston and Texas Central Railroad. Young Patrick started out to study mechanical engineering at A & M College, but switched to the Law School at the University of Texas in 1884 and, after his graduation, hung out his shingle in Austin. Failing to attract many clients, Patrick around 1890 moved on to Houston, where he married a young woman from Louisiana; but his practice continued to languish. At length, after a divorce case in which it was felt that Patrick had obtained fees from both sides, he further alienated the Houston legal community by moving for the impeachment of

84

a Federal judge in Galveston. The judge promptly instructed the district attorney to initiate disbarment proceedings against Patrick, who then prudently decided that New York City offered a wider scope for his talents and so moved there in late 1892.[439]

By all accounts Patrick craved both money and social position; failing twice to achieve these in Texas, he set about obtaining them in New York with calculated deliberation. Neither a smoker nor a drinker, he dressed in excellent taste, became an active worker in the West Side branch of the Young Men's Christian Association and was conspicuous in his attendance at the Fifth Avenue Baptist Church, "John D. Rockefeller's church," as he liked to call it. His wife went back to Louisiana after a short time, with their two daughters, and died there in 1896,[440] whereupon Patrick established himself in a boarding house on West 58th Street and continued to exhibit the characteristics of a cultivated gentleman of some means.

In the months that followed his agreement with Orren Holt, Patrick searched out and interrogated everyone he could find in New York and New Jersey who had known William Marsh Rice and his wife since their marriage and their departure from Houston in June, 1867. His object, of course, was to establish that throughout their married life, despite the farm at Green Brook and the several apartments in New York City, both Rices had considered Texas to be their home. Only if this were true would Elizabeth Baldwin Rice's bequests be valid. As testimony accumulated and, notwithstanding Elizabeth Baldwin Rice's fondness for hearing herself referred to as "Mrs. Rice of Texas" when she was in New York and "Mrs. Rice of New York" when she was in Houston,[441] it became increasingly clear that any case for their having maintained a legal residence in Houston was growing weaker. Patrick did not hesitate to bully some of the ladies whom he was interrogating, particularly young Mrs. Charles Adams and Maria Van Alstyne.[442] More significantly, while Holt, in Houston, was pressing James Baker for a settlement out of court, Patrick became fully aware of the extent of William Marsh Rice's wealth and the terms of his will. In order to learn more about that interesting document, Patrick went to considerable lengths in November, 1899, to make the acquaintance of Charlie Jones.

In an unsophisticated way, Jones undoubtedly had his own dreams of money and fame. Not surprisingly, in view of his youth and rugged good looks, he had considerable success with the ladies and this became expensive. It is doubtful whether he ever seriously considered going back to farming and fruit-growing in Harris County, but he apparently did reflect on the fact that William Marsh Rice was an elderly man and that he, Jones, might find himself without an employer at almost any time. At one point, with the police force in mind, he enrolled in a night school that prepared applicants for the Civil Service; the director, George Gould, found him "one of the most apt and gentlemanly pupils" ever to sign up there. Learning more of Jones' general situation and prospects, Gould told the young man he would do far better by devoting himself to "the old millionaire," and thus being assured of a legacy, than by joining the police force. Before the next school session, Jones reported to Gould that he had taken that advice and that his future was consequently assured. "I don't think Jones ever thought of inheriting any of this money," Gould was to remark later, "until I suggested it to him."[443]

All the evidence points to the fact that Charlie Jones was scrupulously kind toward his elderly employer until the very end, although William Marsh Rice, growing daily more set in his ways, was not always easy to satisfy. One of his habits was to wander about the apartment in the evening as he undressed, leaving his coat in the parlor, his vest in the front "office," his trousers in the bedroom, and his underclothes outside the bathroom door.[444] Jones saw that it was all collected together, brought up wholegrain bread and bouillon from the Diet Kitchen, carried messages back and forth to the telephone in the downstairs hall and opened Mr. Rice's mail. "There was nothing that Mr. Rice did not get into; that is, find his way to, some way. He upset things and went to the bottom of everything."[445] Until March, 1898, Rice wrote most of his own letters in longhand, but in that month the household acquired a typewriter

and Jones thereafter copied out on it what Rice had first draft-
ed, down to the very last inaccuracy. There were apt to be a
good many of these, for William Marsh Rice, like that distin-
guished scholar and Yale president Ezra Stiles, did not hesitate
to spell as he pleased.

His extraordinary capacity for business detail continued un-
diminished, as witness his letters to Arthur Cohn and others:
Henry Oliver, who was in charge of the Merchants and Planters
cottonseed mill, and P. M. Granberry, out at the Rice Ranch.
Privately, Rice complained to Cohn that Granberry had been
a disappointment to him, although given "cart blansh" to do as
he thought best with the ranch property;[446] to Granberry he
repeatedly issued directions about building up the grass and
planting more trees. There is hardly a letter to Cohn which does
not complain about the state of affairs at the Capitol Hotel.
Although in April, 1899, Rice made the observation that the real
value of the brick works lay in the property on which it stood
"when Houston gets to be a great city,"[447] in nearly the same
breath he was wishing to get out of the hotel business, since the
future great city had just doubled his taxes on the Capitol.[448]
Rice was still brooding over the enormity of this last blow when
he wrote to James Baker in June that as far as the hotel was
concerned "I spent money foolishly, thinking Houston would
have a large and rapid growth."[449]

It became increasingly difficult for him to get about. An old
knee injury, dating back to the day some twenty years earlier
when Rice slept through the stop at Dunellen and jumped from
the moving train after it had started up again, troubled him a
good deal. "Pretty near killed himself," had commented a
Green Brook neighbor. "He was just that kind of man that he
thought he would jump."[450] Arthur Cohn wrote that his own
father had greatly benefited under similar circumstances from
alcohol massages,[451] but Rice answered somewhat testily that it
did not seem to help him.[452] For the most part, he continued resolutely cheerful, writing to Cohn in the spring of 1899,
"I think I will have some of my paintings shipped on here. They
are in the way there and they will brighten up things

here . . . .Take those in my two rooms with [the] exception of that Crossing the Desert. There is a smallish one of bathing scene take the one with the Cow & Dog which is in my room . . . Some Books. Send me Shakespeare and ask F. A. Rice to bring from his home Byron and Scotts works . . . .I intended the paintings for the Institute but they can be returned."[453]

For the Institute was never very far from his thoughts. Emanuel Raphael, that remarkable man whom Rice apparently during his lifetime never paid so much as a dollar,[454] corresponded with him regularly about its affairs. In March, 1897, he had reported that the trustees wished for Rice to have his photograph taken and his portrait painted, as well;[455] in November of that year he wrote that a tentative seal had been designed for the Institute and added that, with the arrival of cold weather in Houston, an outbreak of dengue fever had at last come to an end.[456] In 1895 Raphael and Rice had driven out to "old man Albrecht's nursery" in a rented buggy and bought sixty-two young elm trees for the Institute site on Louisiana Street;[457] Raphael, like Rice, was very much concerned about these and wrote in 1898 that he had fenced the property in and engaged a caretaker to live on it, to protect land and trees from vandalism.[458]

Elms and works of art were still as far as William Marsh Rice was prepared to go; he stuck to his original contention that making money was what he did best and that putting up buildings could be better done by younger men when the time came. The Reverend William Leavell, calling on Rice at the Berkshire in October, 1899, in connection with a loan which had been made to the First Presbyterian Church in Houston, urged, as others had done, that it might be well to make a beginning with the actual work of construction, but Rice demurred, adding "and the Institute will have a great deal of money, very much more than you think." The Reverend Leavall recalled afterwards that Rice "took great satisfaction in looking upon himself as a benefactor, the more so because he knew that such was not the usual construction given of his character."[459] The benefactor meanwhile continued to acquire timber lands in

Louisiana as often as those became available, "first class long leaf pine timber" at $2.50 an acre,[460] while at the same time instructing Charlie Jones to write a sharp letter to the United States Express Company, complaining that a box of "Somo" had arrived from Our Home Granula Company with shipping charges of thirty-five cents due. William Marsh Rice had discovered that the shipment had been sent prepaid and wanted his thirty-five cents back.[461]

Arthur Cohn, in Houston, packed up pictures and books; not only Byron and Scott but also *The Last Days of Pompeii, The Vicar of Wakefield,* "Love and Passion" by "Bolzac," Emerson's *Essays,* five volumes of the history of England, Mrs. Heman's *Poetical Works,* Webster's Unabridged Dictionary and *Prominent Women of Texas,* which included a brief biography of Elizabeth Baldwin Rice that claimed kinship for her with the Astors of New York City.[462] In Springfield, Joseph Blinn, the son of Rice's sister Louisa and that Lathrop Blinn who had carried his wages about with him in a "little pretty box," sent his uncle a box of apples and hoped that there would soon be an opening for him with the Merchants and Planters Oil Company.[463] And at the same time, Albert Patrick in New York was not finding it difficult to convince Charlie Jones that it would be a pity if all the old man's money was given away to some orphans' institute in Texas. Patrick's first call at the Berkshire had been in mid-November of 1899, at which time he had told Jones that his name was Smith and chatted with him about Holt's suit in Houston,[464] but on subsequent visits Patrick disclosed his real name and also his designs. Presumably what he suggested at this point was some deflection of Rice's money toward the two of them, and Jones was willing to go along with that.

They made their first move in January, 1900. Walter Wetherbee, the chief clerk at S. M. Swenson and Company, the bank which had handled Rice's affairs in New York for upwards of twenty years, came to see Rice on the afternoon of New Year's Day. A Texan himself, Wetherbee needed $7,000 to take up a debt on property held by him in Texas, but Rice declined to make him the loan.[465] Two days afterwards Jones, who was in the habit of listening to the exchanges between Mr. Rice and his visitors, went to Wetherbee's home in Brooklyn and made the following proposal. "I frequently am writing for Rice, and I can get the old man to sign anything. He is old and dopey. Now, Wetherbee, if you will make out a new will I will substantiate your name as an executor and we can both get our share. You will get one witness for the new will and I'll manage the other. It will be easy. We can slip the new will under the old one and get the old man to sign the wrong paper."[466]

Wetherbee refused. Inevitably, the question was to be asked why he had not reported this conversation to William Marsh Rice. The reasons, he claimed, were twofold: during the previous summer, after one of Rice's regular visits to his safe deposit vault with Wetherbee, the old gentleman had fancied that a thousand-dollar railroad bond was missing and allowed to Charlie Jones that Wetherbee must have taken it. Although the bond turned up in the course of time, the accusation still rankled; furthermore, testified Wetherbee, "I did not go to Rice and tell him about Jones' proposal because I believed Jones had entire control of Rice."[467] There the matter rested, although Wetherbee did report the incident to one of the Swenson brothers and was advised to make a notarized affidavit of his conversation with Jones, which in late March he duly did.[468]

Charlie Jones also became ill, late in March, with what was first described as "catarrhal fever" but soon developed into pneumonia. He was admitted to the Presbyterian Hospital and remained there nearly a month. Charles Carpenter, coming in from Dunellen for his regular Saturday visit with William Marsh Rice, found him in some distress over the prospect of being alone at night and offered to come in from New Jersey every evening and sleep in the apartment until Jones returned; this offer was immediately accepted.[469] He also suggested that he could bring up fresh eggs and vegetables from the country when he came, and this he continued to do for the remainder of Rice's life.[470]

When Jones first became ill, on March 20, 1900, Patrick arranged for his own physician, an elderly man named Walker

Curry who had served as a Confederate medical officer, to treat him. Three days later, when Jones was admitted to the hospital, Rice was anxious to discuss his own health with Curry and within two weeks had placed himself under that practitioner's care. As Patrick had cautioned him to do, saying that Rice was prejudiced against him as a result of what he had heard of the Holt investigations, Curry never mentioned his own acquaintance with the lawyer, on the grounds that it might adversely affect his patient's health.[471] According to Curry, Rice at this time was a "weak old man suffering from partial deafness," with a slow heart action and some swelling in his legs and feet, who overate and took his only exercise by laying down blankets on the floor and rolling about on them for an hour or so. Curry put a stop to this last practice, told Rice to leave off taking pills to improve his hearing and recommended for him a diet consisting mainly of bouillon, calf's foot jelly, peptonized milk, whole wheat bread and Charles Carpenter's New Jersey eggs—in other words, just about what the old gentleman had prescribed for himself. For Charlie Jones, upon his return from the hospital, Curry provided a "tonic" of protoiodide of mercury.[472]

"The least thing, [Mr. Rice] wanted time to reflect. That was his nature, but he was a very good patient, I never had a better," was Curry's opinion. Certainly there was no thought in William Marsh Rice's mind of leaving this world yet; he never lost an opportunity of telling the story of Josiah Hall's long and active life nor of maintaining his own determination to follow suit.[473] In May he sent a note to Wall Street, to let Swenson and Sons know that his books were on their way up from Texas in care of the bank, and he wrote tartly to Mary Brewster, who had chided him once more for not answering her letters, "the fact is I am fond of reading and have a great many persons calling upon me here that probably would not if I was living in Texas and my time is absorbed."[474] The picture which the public was given after his death, of an elderly miser finishing his days in misanthropic solitude, was not an accurate one.

Regretfully, he never met the one member of the family whose determination matched his own, a cousin by the name of

Maria Deane who lived in Ogdensburg, New York. "Cousin Maria," in a clear, regular hand, thanked "Cousin William" in the spring of 1898 for the health magazine which he had so thoughtfully sent to her, and went on to say:

> Years ago I used to say, I intended living to be as old as grandfather Hall was . . . when he died but from the appearance of a Physician's bill just presented at my request, I fear I shall not.
>
> I should really like to meet you, to see one of the family, who, unaided, with his own active brain has accomplished so much. You see I have family pride in a marked degree.[475]

Albert Patrick, for all his careful attention to the details of William Marsh Rice's life history, seems to have overlooked grandfather Hall. In any event, in view of the fact that Rice was eighty-four and not getting about with ease any longer, Patrick felt it increasingly urgent that the old man have an appropriate will. During the summer of 1900, as a result, a document was drawn up, witnessed, and signed with the name of William M. Rice, over the date of June 30. Within a very few months this would come to be known as "the Patrick will."

Earlier during the year, the attorney had begun to practice a reproduction of William Marsh Rice's signature; he tried this out, as it were, with Jones' cooperation, on business letters from Rice to Arthur Cohn and others, which Jones would type up in the usual way and then bring to Patrick for signing.[476] As a further step in his preparations, Patrick had arranged that Jones should from time to time summon two of the lawyer's associates, Morris Meyers, a clerk in Patrick's office who was a registered notary public, and David Short, who at Patrick's suggestion had registered as a commissioner of deeds for Texas, whenever William Marsh Rice had need of either of these services.[477] On the thirtieth of June, 1900, Rice did in fact execute a number of deeds which had been sent on to him from Houston, and both Meyers and Short were present at the Berkshire to take his acknowledgements. Thus, these two could say with entire truthfulness, when called upon, that they had been witnesses to Rice's signature on that date.[478]

To insure himself against the surprise which would be sure to follow when the new will made its appearance, in view of William Marsh Rice's known antipathy for Orren Holt and his associates in general, and for Albert Patrick in particular, Patrick had Jones send him from the Berkshire letters addressed to him containing blank sheets of paper—blank in case the letters were inadvertently returned to Mr. Rice. For this blank paper, once the envelopes were in his hands, Patrick then substituted letters to himself of the appropriate date, over Rice's apparent signature. The existence of a "business correspondence" was thus established.[479] In actuality, Rice and Patrick were only once in each other's presence; during one of the lawyer's evening visits with Jones, Rice opened the door and looked in, only to excuse himself immediately when he saw that "Charlie" had a caller. The next morning, Jones was later to testify, "Mr. Rice wanted to know who that fine looking baldheaded man was that I was talking to last night, and I told him it was a friend of mine."[480]

Meanwhile, whether because, or in spite, of Dr. Curry's attentions—for it was later disclosed that this "guileless old Southern gentleman"[481] who had been in charge of all the Confederate hospitals in Mississippi during the Civil War had never been licensed to practice medicine[482]—William Marsh Rice continued to read the New York *Times,* to belabor Arthur Cohn with instructions about the new awning on the Capitol Hotel and the young live oaks out at the Rice Ranch,[483] and to take a lively interest in the happenings around him. Sometime early in August, Albert Patrick put the inevitable question to Charlie Jones: "Don't you think Rice is living too long for our interests?"[484]

Such at least was Jones' subsequent testimony, but it was also revealed that in the preceding month of July one of his brothers in Texas, William Lafayette Jones, had been asked to obtain chloroform in Galveston, since neither Patrick nor Charlie Jones could have bought it in New York without having a record made of the purchase.[485] At that time William Jones shipped four ounces of chloroform to his brother at 500 Madison Avenue and posted two more, along with two ounces of laudanum, to the same address in mid-August.[486] In August Charlie Jones stopped in at an undertaker's parlor on Houston Street and carried away with him two pamphlets on cremation, which he left on the table where William Marsh Rice habitually transacted his business.[487]

Patrick was meanwhile trying to cover all his bets. He had a will and he was soon to have other assignments of William Marsh Rice's assets to himself, but he had not forgotten that under the terms of his agreement with Orren Holt he stood to receive a fee of $10,000 upon the successful settlement of the lawsuit over Elizabeth Baldwin Rice's will. In the back of his mind was the thought that it might take a good deal of ready cash to see the Rice will of June 30, 1900, through the New York courts. When James Baker had been in New York on business with Mr. Rice earlier in the year, Patrick met with him several times and pressed for a settlement of the will litigation out of court; Baker, who knew that nearly all the evidence coming in was heavily in Rice's favor, rebuffed all such overtures and told William Marsh Rice, sometime late in May, that the suit would in all probability be heard in Galveston the following November.[488] Seeing this avenue closing, Patrick then approached a New Yorker named John E. Whittlesey, who had come out to Texas with the Federal troops and during the late eighteen-sixties became a fairly close friend of William Marsh Rice's, asking Whittlesey to sound Rice out about a settlement of the Holt suit. Rice made it abundantly clear that he considered all the circumstances of his wife's purported last will to be fraudulent and added that if he paid Holt a cent "he would not be able to sleep at nights."[489]

It is of course not possible to say at exactly what point Patrick made up his mind that William Marsh Rice must be gotten out of the way; he seems to have begun by hoping that nature, with a little assistance, would do the job for him, for during the late spring and early summer of 1900 he instructed Jones to start giving the old gentleman some of the mercury pills which had been prescribed for Jones by Curry.[490] A laxative, the medicine weakened Rice and caused him considerable discomfort, but his extraordinarily tough constitution pulled him through each time and he even remarked to Charlie Jones that the pills were doing him good. Patrick then provided more mercury for Jones to administer, but the effect was the same; Rice lost strength, but his mind remained clear and his heart was as sound as ever.

Something which Patrick could not have foreseen finally forced his hand. On the eighth of September, 1900, the upper Gulf Coast was devastated by what was afterwards known as the Great Galveston Hurricane; upwards of 5000 people were killed and untold property destroyed.[491] The city of Houston did not escape; on September 9 Arthur Cohn sent the following telegram to New York: "Hurricane here last night. Roofs all your buildings destroyed and other damages. Wire bank furnish funds quick for repairs."[492]

Most severely damaged of Rice's properties was the Merchants and Planters Oil Company; Henry Oliver, the manager, estimated the losses there at thirty thousand dollars. Two buildings, as well as the main smokestacks, had totally collapsed, which effectively put the mill out of operation. Oliver calculated that the necessary repairs could be finished in ten days, but, since all the bridges to Galveston were also down and could not be rebuilt inside a month, production at the mill would be held up for some time to come.[493]

On September 15, Rice wrote to Oliver that the mill could draw on him for up to $150,000; a first draft for $25,000 should be made on his account at Swenson and Sons at once and a second, for the same amount, ten days later.[494] At that particular time, Rice's balance with Swenson stood at something in the neighborhood of $250,000, an unusually large amount for him to keep on deposit. Patrick, who received regular reports from Jones as to the state of Mr. Rice's business affairs, was well aware of this.

As was his habit, in that third week of September William Marsh Rice had several things on his mind at once. Among his papers are two handwritten versions of an unfinished letter to James Baker, headed only "September 1900" in which he complains at some length about the way his newphew Baldwin

Rice—the same who subsequently served several terms as mayor of Houston—had mismanaged the Rice Ranch. "I was absent or very little in Texas and knew very little of H. B. Rice for several years. Baldwin had got through with his education and he imprest me and I believe others as being very bright. . . . He had bought land to keep his cows between Houston in [the] direction of [the] Ranch. He talked up land and advised me to buy land and start a ranch, I had confidence in his judgment."[495] As a manager, however, Baldwin had turned out to be a disaster; fired long before this letter was written, he had, among other mistakes, located the ranch buildings on land so low that after heavy rains a loaded wagon could not be driven across it and where "shade trees would not thrive."[496]

On the night of September 16, however, three telegrams were sent from Houston which distracted William Marsh Rice from all his other worries. Henry Oliver, James Baker, and T. W. House, Rice's Houston banker, all wired him the news that the already damaged Merchants and Planters had been almost totally destroyed by fire; all three urged its immediate rebuilding. Two days later, Baker estimated that to do so could cost Rice "about two hundred thousand dollars" and another nephew, Benjamin Botts Rice, who was secretary to the Merchants and Planters, notified his uncle that he had sent a draft via House's bank to Swenson and Sons for the amount of $25,000, as Rice had instructed on September 15.[497] With that news, William Marsh Rice's death became certain.

Already distressed by the reports of the hurricane damage, Rice lapsed into a severe depression at the news of the fire. At Jones' urging he had continued to take the tablets containing mercury and when, on Thursday, September 20, Maria Van Alstyne came by to see him,[498] he complained to her of how very ill he was feeling. The preceding year, Mrs. Van Alstyne had seen to it that Rice had had a troublesome wart removed from his face by sending her own doctor around to him; on this occasion she recommended bananas, remarking that they had always been a help to her own digestion.[499] Jones was sent out for bananas that same afternoon and brought back a dozen, which he put into the icebox; the following day, Rice baked five for himself and ate four more raw as well.[500]

Not surprisingly, Rice became acutely ill and dosed himself with still more mercury tablets; the symptoms continued through Friday night and on Saturday Rice was occasionally light-headed. Maria Scott, who came in to clean the apartment two or three times a week, found Mr. Rice still in his bed on Saturday morning; his color was bad and he complained of nausea.[501] By afternoon he was able to sit up in a chair in his usual place by the window and receive Charles and Isabel Carpenter, who had come up from Dunellen on their regular Saturday visit. Rice cried, Isabel Carpenter was to recall, and told them that he had lost over one million dollars in Texas.[502] Dr. Curry also paid a call on the invalid and found him dozing; before Curry left, Rice received a telegram which, he told the doctor, brought more bad news. His heart, according to Curry, was weak but steady; assured that he was doing well, Rice commented "I know that."[503] The draft for $25,000 upon S. M. Swenson and Sons also arrived in New York on Saturday and was brought around to the apartment; Charles Jones, on the grounds that Mr. Rice was not well, was able to put off its presentation at the bank until Monday.[504]

Albert Patrick had not gone near the Berkshire for more than a week, meeting with Jones in other parts of the city so that it would not be possible to associate him with Rice's eventual death. At one of these meetings later on Saturday, Jones told him of the draft's arrival and also that William Marsh Rice was expecting James Baker to be in New York in the very near future.[505] Patrick was also aware that the suit over Elizabeth Baldwin Rice's will was to be heard in November; for his purposes, it would have been disastrous to see the Swenson account depleted just at that moment. "Whatever we do, Mr. Rice cannot be here on Monday because there [are] more of these drafts to follow, and they will consume all the money Mr. Rice has in the bank."[506]

After another bad night, Rice spent most of Sunday sitting at the rear window of his apartment, looking down over Fifth

Avenue, where he could hear the cathedral bells. He remarked once to Charlie Jones that he was thinking of buying an automobile to get around town in.[507] Dr. Curry came by toward eleven and found his patient's breathing rapid but his lungs clear. In the afternoon, Jones tried to get him to drink some medicine mixed in a glass of water, but Rice pronounced the mixture too bitter and spat it out. The dose contained oxalic acid, a vegetable poison which works upon the heart, and Patrick had instructed Jones to make sure that Rice drank it.[508]

It was William Marsh Rice's habit to go to bed around eight o'clock; not surprisingly, he retired much earlier than usual on that Sunday evening and was then so weak that Jones had to carry him across the room from his place by the window.[509] He fell asleep at once and Jones went out to get his own supper and also to report to Patrick that the attempt to administer the oxalic acid had been a failure. Patrick then gave him the bottle of chloroform and told Jones exactly how it was to be used. He also pointed out, not for the first time, that "if Mr. Rice had poisoned his wife or caused her to be poisoned, it would be no sin to put him out of the way."[510] This was not a line of thought that originated with Patrick; it had been rather heavily suggested by the Baldwins, at the time that Patrick was taking evidence from them, and they were to repeat the insinuation to newspaper reporters in the days immediately to come.[511]

Patrick returned to his boarding house, dined early, and spent an hour or so accompanying two of his fellow lodgers, a Mrs. Elliot and her daughter, Mabel, on the piano while the ladies practiced some hymns before going on to a Christian Endeavor meeting later in the evening.[512] Charlie Jones, returning to the apartment on Madison Avenue, took a small sponge which William Marsh Rice used for cleaning his own clothes, placed it inside a towel pinned into the shape of a cone, as Patrick had showed him how to do, and poured about two ounces of chloroform into the sponge. Rice was still apparently asleep and had not moved. Jones put the cone over his face and left the room.

Within a few moments the doorbell began to ring. It rang for some time, was silent for a quarter of an hour, and then rang again. Downstairs in the apartment house lobby, two ladies from Galveston who were old friends of William Marsh Rice's had come to pay a Sunday evening call. The elevator attendant, going upstairs to see if Mr. Rice could receive them, got no response and returned to say that Rice's secretary-valet appeared to have gone out. The ladies waited for a short while, sent the boy upstairs a second time without success, and left word that they would call again the next day.[513] Inside the apartment, Jones waited thirty minutes after he had left Rice's bedroom and then went in to find that his employer was dead. Cone and sponge remained undisturbed; he took them into the kitchen and burned them.[514]

According to Paul Teich, the elevator attendant, about three-quarters of an hour after the ladies had departed, Charlie Jones came downstairs and asked that someone be sent for Dr. Curry. After the doctor's arrival, Jones came down again, told Teich that Mr. Rice was dead and put through a call from the lobby telephone. Shortly afterward, Albert Patrick came in and went up to Rice's apartment.[515] It was then about nine o'clock.

At ten o'clock that evening, an undertaker named Charles Plowright was summoned to 500 Madison Avenue. Albert Patrick told him that the deceased had always expressed the wish to be cremated and that the ceremony was therefore to take place on the following day, Monday. Plowright was obliged to tell him that this could not be done, as the crematory furnaces required at least twenty-four hours preparation.[516] It was the one thing that Patrick had not thought of. As an alternative, he ordered that the body should meanwhile be embalmed that same night.[517]

Monday morning at around eleven o'clock, a young man later identified as the same David Short who had signed his name as a witness to the will of June 30, 1900, presented a check for $25,000 to the cashier at S. M. Swenson and Sons. Dated the twenty-second of September, it was made out to Abert T. Patrick and bore the signature "William M. Rice." The cashier, who knew that Mr. Rice rarely wrote a check so large and who furthermore disliked the look of the signature, carried it to

Walter Wetherbee. Wetherbee, not surprisingly, had become exceedingly circumspect in everything that concerned Rice; he agreed that the signature was not convincing and called attention to the fact that although made out to "Abert" the check had been endorsed "Albert" T. Patrick.

The cashier accordingly informed Short that the check, because of its erroneous endorsement, could not be certified. Short left the bank and was back within a half-hour with the correct endorsement, but by this time Eric Swenson had come into his office and he agreed that Mr. Rice's signature was suspect. After comparing it with other signed documents in the bank's vaults, he instructed the cashier to telephone the Berkshire and receive personal confirmation as to the authenticity of the check. Jones, who was evidently waiting by the hall telephone, replied immediately and protested that it was good, but Swenson put through a second call and insisted on receiving verbal confirmation from Mr. Rice himself. Only then did Jones reveal that Rice was dead. Swenson, in consequence, informed Short that the check could not be honored.[518]

At about the same time, James Baker, in Houston, received a telegram signed "C. F. Jones" which read, "Mr. Rice died 8 o'clock last night under care physician. Death certificate old age weak heart diarrahue [sic]. Left instructions to be interred at Milwaukee with wife. Funeral ten a.m. tomorrow at 500 Madison Avenue. When will you come."[519] The death of an eighty-four-year-old man cannot have been entirely unexpected; Baker wired Jones that Rice's papers and the keys to the apartment should be turned over to the banker Norman Meldrum, who was at that time staying at the Waldorf-Astoria; he then telephoned Frederick Allyn Rice with the news. It was agreed that Baker should go directly to New York to begin the settlement of Rice's affairs and that Frederick Rice would join him there after attending the burial in Waukesha.[520]

It was the consistent good fortune of the Rice Institute that William Marsh Rice chose as his associates men of unusual shrewdness and integrity. Without them, all of Rice's expressed satisfaction at having made foolproof arrangements for the future of his "baby"[521] might have served only as the occasion for eventual irony. Eric Swenson, who was disturbed by the incident of the check, went around that same afternoon to consult James W. Gerard, a young attorney in the law firm of Bowers and Sands. On Gerard's advice, Swenson telegraphed to Baker in Houston, "Mr. Rice died last night under very suspicious circumstances. His body will be cremated tomorrow morning at nine o'clock. Interment at Waukesha."[522]

Baker and Frederick Rice immediately sent back an order to stop the cremation proceedings and started for New York together. Gerard meanwhile kept up his inquiries well into Monday night; he went first to the district attorney's office; next, to call upon Dr. Curry; and lastly, accompanied by a detective, had an interview with Albert Patrick at Patrick's boarding house near midnight. There for the first time Patrick disclosed the facts which were to stun all of William Marsh Rice's associates: firstly, that Rice's will of 1896, in which the Rice Institute had been named as residuary legatee, had been superseded by the will of June 30, 1900, in which Albert T. Patrick was so designated, and, secondly, that Patrick held a general assignment as of September 21, 1900, by which all of William Marsh Rice's property, whether in money or securities, was turned over to him in exchange for an annual payment of $10,000 during Rice's lifetime,[523] as "the old man had tired of life and had tired of business."[524] Swenson and Gerard were not alone in finding these facts unsettling; when they were brought to the attention of the district attorney's office, an immediate autopsy was ordered. After a funeral service read in the Berkshire apartment by a curate of Calvary Church on the morning of Tuesday, September 25, William Marsh Rice's body was removed to the city morgue, where its vital organs were removed for examination.[525] The following day, September 26, the body was cremated at Fresh Pond on Long Island, in the presence of Dr. Curry, Charles Jones, Frederick Allyn Rice, who had arrived from Houston that same morning, and a considerable number of newspaper reporters.[526]

For the press, not surprisingly, was having a field day. The death of a millionaire recluse was good for a certain amount of copy in itself, along with all the details, real or fancied, of the old gentleman's way of living, his eccentricities, and his dislike of publicity. The entrance of the district attorney's office into the picture provided reporters with fresh fuel; by Friday one evening newspaper already carried a vigorous statement made in Springfield by Charlotte Rice McKee, who did not hesitate to declare that her brother had been "murdered for his millions." "William was in excellent health. My grandfather lived to be 101 and William often said he expected to live that long."[527]

James Baker, with the prudence of the legal profession, was not yet prepared to go that far in public. What concerned him was the fortune which had been intended for the realization of Mr. Rice's Institute and which now appeared, under the terms of the will of June 30, to be lost to it forever. By the terms of the "Patrick will," the Rice Institute was to receive a legacy of only $250,000, subject to the condition that it had not previously been assigned gifts and properties equal to that sum. In effect, on these terms the Institute would not get a cent; Baker, as a trustee, was well aware that the endowment already amounted to a great deal more than $250,000 and, what was more important, he knew that William Marsh Rice himself could have reckoned its worth almost to a penny.[528] For Rice to have inserted such a clause in a will made less than three months ago was unthinkable.

During the next few weeks, James Baker can almost be said to have saved the Rice Institute single-handed. By October 2 he was writing to the board of directors in Houston for authority to use his own discretion in employing counsel and gathering testimony to fight the Patrick will. James Gerard had laid a certain amount of groundwork, and Baker, working with the cooperation of the district attorney's office, accumulated sufficient evidence that on October 4, 1900, a fortnight after William Marsh Rice's death, Albert Patrick and Charles Jones were arrested for forgery and sent to the Tombs.[529] The indictment was based on the checks which Patrick had had presented for payment at Swenson's and at the Fifth Avenue Trust Company,[530] but it immediately became apparent that the "Patrick will," the general assignment to Patrick of Rice's entire estate, and even some of the salary checks which had been sent to Arthur Cohn in July and August while Patrick was perfecting his reproduction of Rice's signature, were fraudulent as well.

"I am convinced that a bold attempt was made to criminally get possession of Mr. Rice's vast estate. Other disclosures are coming equally startling as those already made," announced Baker the day after the two arrests.[531] The press could hardly believe its good fortune. "Police Scout Theory of Murder" proclaimed the New York *Tribune* on October 6.

While editors rejoiced and handwriting experts wrangled over the signatures on those checks amounting to a total of $225,000 which Patrick claimed William Marsh Rice had drawn to him on September 22, the trustees of the Rice Institute, not to be outdone, filed the deed to the Capitol Hotel property which had reverted to the Institute upon Rice's death as well as a petition to change its name to the Rice Hotel.[532] More significantly, on October 27 the coroner's office in New York reported that arsenic, which was attributable to the embalming fluid, as well as a considerable amount of mercury, which was not, had been found in Rice's vital organs.[533] In the opinion of the chemist who had made the analysis, the quantity of bichloride of mercury present was sufficient to have caused death.[534]

Albert Patrick's motives, from first to last, were calculated and perfectly clear. Charlie Jones, however, seems to have had little initiative of his own, being susceptible instead to whatever stronger personality went to work on him. Capable of considerable patience and apparent real concern for William Marsh Rice over several years, as Dr. Curry among others had not failed to observe,[535] he was also capable of putting the cone containing chloroform over his employer's face. At no time, in prison or out of it, did Albert Patrick admit to any of the charges brought against him; Jones, on the other hand, whether upon the promptings of his own conscience or because he believed that he was going to be made the scapegoat, broke down after the coroner's report was made public and sent word to the prosecuting attorney that he wished to make a statement. In the presence of Baker and others, Jones then confessed to the entire scheme whereby he and Patrick were to gain control of Rice's wealth and went on to swear that on the evening of Sunday, September 23, he had seen Patrick hold the towel containing chloroform over Rice's nose and mouth until the old man had ceased to breathe.[536]

After he had been taken back to the Tombs that night, Charlie Jones made his first suicide attempt, hacking at his throat with a penknife which Patrick had passed through from his neighboring cell after hearing of the confession, with the plea, "I have two children; . . . what will become of them, if anything happened to me?"[537] Removed to Bellevue Hospital, Jones made another confession a few days later, more or less along the lines of the first, in which he still maintained that Patrick had done the actual chloroforming.[538]

The publicity which William Marsh Rice had so studiously avoided during his lifetime had caught up with him with a vengeance after his death. One of its results was the unexpected emergence of a whole branch of Rice relatives who were living in Stone County, Missouri, "in abject poverty."[539] When it was told, their story was one marked by considerable irony, for these Stone County Rices turned out to be the children of that dashing brother, David Rice, who had last been heard from with Hood's Texans in Tennessee.

> My father's name is David Rice. He was born in the State of Mass. He had three brothers and two sisters, their names is William M. Rice, Caleb Rice, Frederick, Louise and Charlotte Rice. I am not able to tell you where they reside, who they married, or how many descendants they may have, at the age of manhood my father married a young lady of Springfield, Mass. 2 Sons were born to them, William A. and David Rice. My Father's wife died, leaving his two sons with his parents. He come west. He was commissioned Col. of a company of Rangers by Sam Houston and afterwards was made Col. by the U.S. and was in the largest Battles of the Mexican war. Including the capture of the city of Mexico, during those years his brother William M. Rice came out to texas & established a firm known as the Firm of Rice and Nickles

of Houston, texas, his brother Caleb & Fredrick came out to texas, But caleb soon went back to Mass., but Fredrick married in texas and was there until on or about the commencement of the late war o[f] the Rebellion. My father his two sons and brothers all got seperated and my father has never herd from any of them since although He has written many letters. He come to the conclusion that they were all dead & and I am shure they thought him dead. After the war my father settled here in Missouri and married Miss Pauline Schlicht, formerly of Pilot Mound, Iowa. Five children were born to them, three sons and 2 daughters, two of them is dead and 3 are living & I am the oldest one of them that is alive. All three of us are living here at Radical. Our mother is living here with us. Father died the 30 of December 1899, being a few years older than his brother William M. Rice.[540]

So wrote the oldest of David Rice's surviving sons by this second marriage, Benjamin Franklin Rice, to Captain McCluskey of the New York Detective Bureau; allowing for what he could not have been expected to know, his facts were in the main accurate. The newspapers, making the most of this timely appearance of long-lost heirs, dug out further details for their interested readers. Benjamin Rice and his brother and sister all lived in primitive houses "built of hewn logs, with clumsy outdoor chimneys laid up of rough yellow boulders." These houses had no windows, carpets, or stoves, and the chairs and bedsteads in them had been made by hand, while harness hung from pegs beside the door along with calendars advertising stock feed and patent medicine. From David Rice each of his surviving children had inherited 160 acres of farmland;[541] they were never told of the existence of a wealthy uncle.

While gossip in Stone County must have been soaring to new heights, the district attorney's office in New York continued to pile up evidence against Albert Patrick. Released on bail through the efforts of a well-to-do brother-in-law in St. Louis, he was immediately rearrested on the charge of first degree murder on the strength of affidavits supplied by Charles Jones and the examining chemist of the coroner's office and arraigned on March 26, 1901.[542] Three days later Morris Myers and David Short were also arrested, on the grounds that they had committed perjury in acting as witnesses to a will which they knew to be fraudulent.[543]

Patrick's attorneys lost no time in putting Mrs. Elliot and her daughter on the stand to testify that, at the moment when the murder was being committed, the accused was playing hymns in the parlor at West Fifty-Eighth Street.[544] Faced with this unshakeable evidence, and after a second suicide attempt in the interval, Jones then made a third and final confession in which he admitted that, upon Patrick's instructions, it was he who had chloroformed William Marsh Rice.[545] On April 23, 1901, Patrick was indicted for murder as well as for forgery, in the longest indictment ever drawn up by the New York district attorney's office.[546] The court records of his trial and appeals eventually ran to something over three thousand pages,[547] a fascinating study of criminal law at work for anyone with the curiosity and the time to go through them. The essential point was simple: under the code of criminal proceedings, the testimony of an accomplice must be "corroborated by such other evidence as would tend to connect the defendant with the commission of the crime." The forged will of June 30, the false general assignment, the fraudulent checks, the letters prepared by Patrick and Jones to establish the appearance of a correspondence between Rice and Patrick when in fact the two had never met aside from the single accidental encounter in Jones' room, and the procuring of chloroform from Galveston through the assistance of William Lafayette Jones, were all held to constitute such evidence, and the defense then fell back on the contention that William Marsh Rice had been in fact already dead when the cone of chloroform was placed over his face. That congestion of his lungs which had been duly noted at the time of the autopsy was, the defense maintained, in fact due to natural causes. Old Dr. Curry, however, their principal witness, more or less contradicted himself by first swearing that Rice's death was in his opinion a natural one and then admitting that he had found no congestion in his patient's lungs on the morning of his death.[548] Patrick was found guilty on March 26, 1902, and sentenced to die in the electric chair. Charlie Jones was allowed to return to

Texas in the company of his brother, William. There he disappeared from sight until 1954 when, a solitary and aging man, he shot himself in his Baytown home.[549]

Sensation seekers, who packed the courtroom from the beginning, had not failed to note an announcement carried by New York newspapers in April, 1901: an auction "of peculiar interest," it read, was to be held at Silo's Art Galleries in Liberty Street. By order of the temporary administrator of the estate of William Marsh Rice, "assorted furniture and personal belongings," including the folding bed "in which the millionaire had died," a set of parlor chairs inlaid with mother-of-pearl, a pair of onyx paperweights, Rice's spectacle case and his two sets of false teeth, went under the hammer,[550] and purchasers were told that they might "charge people 25 cents each" to look at Mr. Rice's effects.[551]

Those who had no taste for being elbowed by the crowds could stay at home and let the New York *Times* inform them that on the first day of his trial Albert Patrick had appeared in court wearing a new frock coat, light trousers, and patent leather boots.[552] Somewhat portly, balding, looking older than his thirty-four years, he betrayed his nervousness only by occasionally pulling at his reddish beard.[553] When the verdict against him was returned, however, he was entirely at his ease, and two days later announced from prison his engagement to Mrs. Addie Francis, the personable widow at whose boarding house he had been living since his wife's death; Mrs. Francis had gratified reporters and readers alike by collapsing in a dead faint after the verdict was brought in.[554]

The defense had not hesitated to fight back with every weapon they could lay their hands on; James Baker, grieving over his eldest son's recent death from pneumonia,[555] heard himself described in court as the real villain of the piece. The Houston attorney, it was charged, had invented Jones' "confession" so that he himself might gain control of the Rice fortune. "We've seen it amply proved that everyone of the Texas contingent had his price."[556] Shortly after Patrick's sentencing, the millionairess Hetty Green, no mean eccentric herself, marched into the police station nearest her home and demanded a permit for a pistol on the grounds that the wealthy were no longer safe. She denied strenuously any feelings of fear: "The only two things in this world I am afraid of . . . are lightning and a religious lawyer."[557]

The religious lawyer, meanwhile, had already filed an appeal which effectively stayed his execution. The Court of Appeals reaffirmed his conviction, however, although by a vote of only four to three, on June 9, 1905, and he was resentenced to die the week of August 7. A new appeal was denied for the second time in November and Patrick's execution was set for January of 1906.[558] By this time, an organization in New York City known as the Medico-Legal Society had taken up Patrick's cause, possibly at the prompting of his wealthy brother-in-law, and arrived at the conclusion that chloroform had not, after all, been the cause of William Marsh Rice's death.

> The Committee are agreed, after carefully analyzing all the medical and other evidence furnished upon this case, that Mr. Rice did not die from chloroform poisoning, and furthermore, that no chloroform was administered by Jones, as stated by him to Mr. Rice while the said Rice was living, because it would have been impossible for the towel cone containing chloroform to remain unsupported upon the face of Rice, while asleep. It is also the opinion of the Committee, without exception, that no chloroform was ever administered to Rice by Jones, as stated by him, because it would have been impossible not to have detected the odor of chloroform either in the room occupied by the deceased or from the body, as the amount of chloroform employed, as alleged, would have saturated the beard of deceased and retained the odor for many hours, however thoroughly the apartments may have been ventilated.[559]

All that is lacking is the story that Baker put Jones up to it; nonetheless, whether as a result of these dubious findings or because three out of the seven judges of the Court of Appeals had dissented from the decision affirming sentence, on December 20, 1906, New York's Governor Higgins commuted the death sentence to life imprisonment. Patrick and his backers continued their fight for a full pardon and six years later this was granted by the then Governor of the State, John A. Dix, on November 27, 1912.[560] Before departing for Oklahoma, where he was to live on until 1940 scraping up a living as counsel to an oil company when he was not selling automobiles and air-conditioners,[561] Albert Patrick could have read that on the twelfth anniversary of William Marsh Rice's death, September 23, 1912, the Rice Institute had opened its doors in Houston.

During the temporary abatement of both suit and countersuit in the matter of Elizabeth Baldwin Rice's will that followed Rice's death, Orren Holt had time to think things over. The bulk of the testimony which by then had been taken, north and south, indicated that there was little hope of establishing that the Rices' residence had in fact been in Texas, and that Mrs. Rice's will would therefore become valueless. Holt had also by that time developed the political ambitions that would result, in 1902, in his election as mayor of Houston. Accordingly, on February 6, 1902, he settled out of court with Rice's executors for the sum of $200,000[562] which satisfied all but a handful of Elizabeth Baldwin Rice's legatees, which last included, to no one's surprise, the aggrieved Laura Geddes Morton.[563] Added to this sum were the bequests made by William Marsh Rice to his brother, Frederick, his two sisters, Charlotte and Minerva, and his nephew William Marsh Rice, Jr., plus lawyers' fees in New York and Houston and executors' commissions, all of which ran to a charge against the estate of something over a million dollars.[564] Nevertheless, when the residue, together with properties already held by the Institute, was placed in the hands of James Baker and the other trustees on April 29, 1904, they found themselves in charge of assets totalling $4,631,259.08.[565]

Where there might now have been an end to William Marsh Rice's story, there was, of course, only a beginning. The history of the Rice Institute thereafter can be traced step by step through the relevant documents when its time comes to be written. Between that day in April 1904, however, and the one in September 1912 when the first students—seventy-seven in number—presented themselves at the first lecture, lie eight years which may well have been the most critical in the Institute's history, when Baker, Raphael (who was at long last, under specifications set out in Rice's will, put on the payroll), and the other trustees taxed their ingenuity to bring about what the founder, not without a certain sense of humor, had left to the efforts of "younger men."

Clearly the immediate need of the trustees was for an educator of stature who would serve as president of Mr. Rice's Institute, and after careful consideration they found him in the person of Edgar Odell Lovett among the faculty members of Princeton University. Here once again the connection with William Marsh Rice was a direct one, for it was during those years at Princeton which he owed to his uncle that William Marsh Rice, Jr., had come to know an undergraduate named Woodrow Wilson, and it was to Wilson, since 1902 the president of the university, that the trustees addressed themselves in their search for a head.

Lovett, like Rice before him, undertook a careful study of other great centers of learning during a twelve-months' journey that carried him as far afield as Edinburgh and Tokyo. Long before this, however, the trustees had realized that Mr. Rice's original choice of a six-acre site on Louisiana Street was no longer adequate to the needs of the Institute: in agreement with Lovett, they settled on the location where the present Rice University stands, a rough polygon of approximately three hundred acres, bordered along one side by an unpaved country road which ran south and west of the city in a continuation of Main Street.[566] "In all directions in the immediate neighborhood of the town the prospects are the same—stretch upon stretch of flat prairie, covered with flowers in spring; brown with parched grass after the summer; full of shallow ponds and swamps; browsed over by cattle; its horizons interrupted by belts of trees along the creeks and bayous, belts that become woods on the drained grounds near the bigger watercourses."[567]

With little to interrupt that prairie except a few scattered farms, the next logical step was to lay a spur of the San Antonio and Aransas Pass Railroad on to the new campus and bring in construction material over it.[568] Lovett, fresh from Bologna, Leipzig, and the Trans-Siberian, joined with the trustees in asking Ralph Adams Cram, a Bostonian also associated with

Princeton, to draw up an overall plan for the buildings of the Institute; oddly enough, the architect never visited the site of his enormous new project before construction was begun,[569] but contented himself with studies of the climate, geography, and physical attributes of the Gulf Coast.

As a result of his researches Cram seized upon northern Italy and the Dalmatian coast in his search after an equivalent for the conditions of Harris County. "All of the courts have been so arranged that the prevailing winds blow unobstructed into them. . . . In the use of color the effort has been to secure a dominant interesting note, which in southern sunlight should be neither glaring because of its lightness nor offensive because of the intensity of its color."[570] Eschewing his favorite Gothic style for the round arch of Dalmatia and Spain, Cram had his brick made of special clays and put the contractor to so much difficulty in specifying different kinds of colored marble that the Institute finally bought a whole quarry in Oklahoma as the simplest solution to its problems.

Certain of the original plans had eventually to be abandoned, including the Persian gardens with their marble reflecting basins, which were something less than appropriate, as indeed William Marsh Rice could have told Cram, in a climate noted for its mosquitoes and its malaria. Yet even the young Julian Huxley, one of that group of very able men who, through President Lovett's efforts, were to guide the Institute through its first years, found the overall effect impressive. "Across from the car-line by a ramshackle wooden farmhouse, we were confronted by an extraordinary spectacle, as of palaces in fairy-story. The Administration Building [now Lovett Hall] was before us, looking exactly as if it had risen miraculously out of the earth . . . . Here it stood, brilliant, astounding, enduring: rising out of the barren brown prairie which extended, unbroken save for a belt of trees, to the horizon and far beyond the horizon."[571]

For all his gentle ridicule of the spittoons and oratory of Houston, Huxley was quick to grasp the significance of the Rice Institute. Writing in 1918 for English readers, he reminded them that nothing in the European experience was an adequate preparation for the America that lay behind a narrow Eastern strip of Europeanized cities.

> If this civilisation ever reaches its maturity, it will be a very different thing from any production of Europe. It starts with enormous prosperity and still far from developed resources in land, in minerals, in water-power. It has for basis a democracy which has not had to struggle up to the light against the vested rights and accumulated weight of aristocracy, and which, if it is more careless, is less warped than ours. It is permeated with a restlessness, a divine discontent: the days of simple pioneering, whether made visible in the strings of prairie schooners or in the violent growth of young towns from nothing, are over for good; and now, all over the middle West, is a feeling that material prosperity is not enough, a sense of something lacking—something, they know not what . . . . And, finally, the new civilisation starts from a level of education, combined with a degree of leisure to pursue and enjoy the fruits of education, that is a new thing in history. It is the fashion to belittle American higher education . . . . But two essential facts are forgotten. One is that the average level is high—that somehow or other a much larger percentage of men and women get some sort of higher education than is the case in England. This would not of itself mean much, if it were not for the second fact—namely that the level, both of the best and of the average, is being continually raised.[572]

"An uninstructed Englishman," Huxley goes on to say, might have expected that in a region only a few years removed from the frontier, the trustees of the Rice Institute would have settled for a modest technical college or "little provincial University"; that they had not was to his way of thinking the fact most worth remembering about Mr. Rice's Institute, "because a true University begins to be in touch with the universal."[573] Sixty years afterward, it hardly seems necessary to point out that this was what William Marsh Rice had in mind.

DAVID RICE

The father of William Marsh Rice
from a photograph in the Rice
Papers, Fondren Library,
Rice University.

JOSIAH HALL

The maternal grandfather of William
Marsh Rice from a photograph in
the Rice Papers.

WILLIAM MARSH RICE

From a copy of an original oil painting of William Marsh Rice at the age of 34 years. Presented to the Rice Institute by William M. Rice, Jr., Dec., 1908.

MARGARET BREMOND RICE

The original of this portrait of the first Mrs. William Marsh Rice is now in the Archives of Fondren Library, Rice University.

THE RICE-NICHOLS-CHERRY HOUSE

The Rice Mansion as restored by the Harris County Heritage Society and moved to Sam Houston Historical Park. (Photo courtesy Harris County Heritage Society.)

ELIZABETH BALDWIN RICE
(The second Mrs. William Marsh
Rice)

The Madison Avenue structure in
which the last Rice apartment was
located (from the Newspaper Files,
William Marsh Rice Papers, Fondren
Library, Rice University).

ALBERT T. PATRICK
(From the Newspaper Files.)

CHARLES F. JONES
(From the Newspaper Files.)

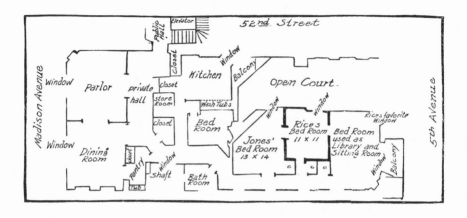

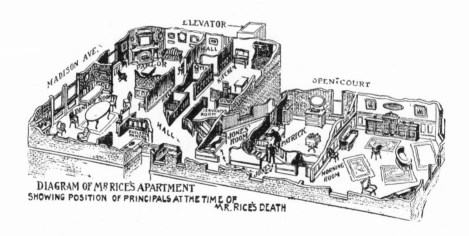

DIAGRAM OF MR RICE'S APARTMENT
SHOWING POSITION OF PRINCIPALS AT THE TIME OF MR. RICE'S DEATH

TWO VERSIONS OF THE FLOOR PLAN OF THE RICE APARTMENT AT THE TIME OF
RICE'S MURDER. (From the Newspaper Files.)

A Newspaper Artist's drawing of EMANUEL RAPHAEL during the murder trial. *New York World,* Jan. 31, 1902.

A Newspaper Artist's drawing of CAPTAIN JAMES A. BAKER during the murder trial.
New York World, Jan. 29, 1902.

MRS. ADDIE M. FRANCIS, witness for
the defense in the Patrick trial —
later married to Patrick. (From the
Newspaper Files.)

ALBERT T. PATRICK at the time his
sentence was commuted to life
imprisonment by Governor Higgins
of New York. (From the
Newspaper Files.)

The First Board of Trustees of the Rice Institute

Left to right: B. B. Rice, Edgar O. Lovett, Emanuel Raphael, William Marsh Rice, Jr., J. E. McAshan, C. Lombardi, and James A. Baker. (Research Center Fondren Library.)

NOTES

NOTES

1. Timothy Dwight, *Travels in New England and New York,* ed. Barbara Miller Solomon (Cambridge: The Belknap Press of Harvard University, 1969), Vol. I, p.231.

2. Report of the Secretary of War, Communicating, 29th Congress, 1st Session, Senate, No. 344. Ordered to lie on table and printed, 14 May, 1846: ordered that 1000 additional copies be printed for use of Senate, 18 May 1846, pp. 23-27.

3. G. C. Bliss, in the Houston *Chronicle,* March 14, 1916.

4. O. P. Allen, "The Late William Marsh Rice," Springfield *Daily Republican,* May 24, 1901, p. 12, cols. 4-5.

5. Report of the Secretary of War, op. cit.

6. Timothy Dwight, *Travels in New England,* I, 231.

7. Ibid.

8. Alfred Minot Copeland, ed., *A History of Hampden County, Massachusetts* (n.p.: The Century Memorial Publishing Company, 1902), Vol. II, pp. 261-262.

9. Clifton Johnson, *Hampden County, 1636-1936* (New York: The American Historical Society, Inc., 1936), Vol. I, p.279.

10. Timothy Dwight, *Travels in New England,* II, 230.

11. Ibid.

12. William Marsh Rice to Charlotte Rice McKee (?), March 23, 1899 (William Marsh Rice Papers in the Fondren Library, Rice University, Houston, Texas).

13. Andrew Forest Muir, "William Marsh Rice and His Institute," a paper read before the Historical Society of the Rice Institute, November 13, 1958, p.2 (Andrew Forest Muir Papers in the Fondren Library, Rice University, Houston, Texas).

14. Ibid.

15. Josiah Gilbert Holland, *History of Western Massachusetts* (Springfield: Samuel Bowles and Co., 1855), Vol. II, pp. 122-123.

16. Andrew Forest Muir, "William Marsh Rice and His Institute," p.1.

17. *Centennial Souvenir of the New England Conference and of Springfield Methodism.* Published on the occasion of the One Hundredth Session of the Conference, held in Asbury First Church, Springfield, Mass., April, 1896 (Springfield: Rev. Charles Tilton, publisher, 1896), p.12.

18. Ibid., p.16.

19. Ibid.

20. Andrew Forest Muir, "William Marsh Rice and His Institute," p.2.

21. A. M. Copeland, *History of Hampden County*, II, 116.

22. G. C. Bliss, Houston *Chronicle*, March 14, 1916.

23. William Orr, *The History of the Classical High School, Springfield, Massachusetts* (Springfield: Classical High School Alumni Association, 1936), p. 19.

24. A. M. Copeland, *History of Hampden County*, II, 116.

25. Charles Wells Chapin, *History of the "Old High School" on School Street, Springfield, from 1828 to 1840* (Springfield: Press of the Springfield Printing and Binding Co., 1890), p.9.

26. William Orr, *History of Classical High School*, pp. 18-19.

27. Ibid., p.19.

28. Charles Wells Chapin, *History of "Old High School,"* pp. 28-29.

29. Andrew Forest Muir, "William Marsh Rice and His Institute," p.3; O. P. Allen, "The Late William Marsh Rice," Springfield *Daily Republican*, May 24, 1901, p.12, cols. 4-5; Charles Wells Chapin, *Sketches of the Old Inhabitants and Other Citizens of Old Springfield of the Present Century* (Springfield: Press of the Springfield Printing and Binding Co., 1893), pp.89-90.

30. David Sherman, *History of the Wesleyan Academy at Wilbraham, Mass., 1817-1890* (Boston: The McDonald and Gill Co., 1893), pp.11, 69, and 71-73.

31. William Marsh Rice to Charlotte Rice McKee, June 30, 1900 (Rice Litigation Papers, Fondren Library, Rice University, Houston, Texas).

32. O. P. Allen, "The Late William Marsh Rice."

33. Probate Case Papers of Hampden County, Massachusetts (MS in Registry of Probate, Springfield), File 9340.

34. William Marsh Rice to Charlotte Rice McKee (?), March 23, 1899 (William Marsh Rice Papers, Fondren Library).

35. Ibid.

36. "Mr. Clark's interview with Charlotte McKee," Springfield, Mass., February 19-20, 1904 (Rice Litigation Papers, Fondren Library).

37. Testimony of Charlotte Rice McKee, Springfield, Massachusetts, March 31 - April 6, 1904 (Rice Litigation Papers, Fondren Library).

38. Ibid.

39. "Death of a Centenarian," Dedham, Massachusetts, *Gazette*, July 21, 1855, p.2, col.1.

40. "The Family of William Marsh Rice," by Frank McKee, enclosure in letter from Frank McKee to Edgar Odell Lovett, April 3, 1913 (Edgar Odell Lovett Papers, Fondren Library, Rice University, Houston, Texas).

41. Application of Josiah Hall to U.S. War Department for pension, under act of Congress, 7 June 1832. Walpole, 22 August 1832 (Revolutionary

Pension; MS in the National Archives, file 29,865).

42. Ibid.

43. J. L. Edwards to Josiah Hall, September 25, 1820 (National Archives, Record Group No. ISA).

44. William Ellis to James L. Edwards, August 9, 1846 (National Archives, Record Group No. ISA).

45. "Schedule of all the property of the within named applicant for the continuance of his pension" (National Archives, Record Group No. ISA).

46. Springfield *Republican and Journal,* July 29, 1837, 3*d* and November 18, 1837, 3*d.*

47. Andrew Forest Muir, "William Marsh Rice and His Institute," p.3.

48. Mortgages of Personal Property, Springfield, Massachusetts (MS in City Clerk's office, Springfield), I, 303.

49. James A. Baker, Jr., "Reminiscences of the Founder," *The Rice Institute Pamphlet,* Vol. XVIII, No. 3 (July 1931), p.130.

50. Andrew Forest Muir, "William Marsh Rice and His Institute," p.4.

51. Springfield *Republican and Journal,* September 26, 1837.

52. Ibid, June 3, 1837.

53. B. H. Carroll, Jr., ed. *Standard History of Houston Texas From a Study of the Original Sources* (Knoxville, Tennessee: H. W. Crew, 1910), pp.26-27.

54. Ibid., p.33

55. Marguerite Johnston, *A Happy Worldly Abode: Christ Church Cathedral, 1839-1964* (Houston: Cathedral Press, 1964), p.12.

56. T. R. Fehrenbach, *Lone Star: A History of Texas and the Texans* (New York: Macmillan, 1968), p.282.

57. James A. Baker, "The Patrick Case," privately printed, August 6, 1954; Andrew Forest Muir, "William Marsh Rice, His Life and Death," a paper read before the Harris County Historical Society, September 6, 1955, p.4 (Andrew Forest Muir Papers, Fondren Library).

58. William Marsh Rice to Mary C. Brewster, January 8, 1899 (William Marsh Rice Papers, Fondren Library).

59. Andrew Forest Muir, "William Marsh Rice and His Institute," p.5.

60. B. H. Carroll, Jr., *History of Houston,* p.71.

61. M. Johnston, *Happy Worldly Abode,* p.19.

62. Ibid., p.16.

63. Ibid., p.14.

64. B. H. Carroll, Jr., *History of Houston,* pp.46-47.

65. Ibid., p.30.

66. Ibid., p.66.

67. Deed Records of Harris County (County Clerk's office, Houston), D, 268-269.

68. Andrew Forest Muir, "William Marsh Rice and His Institute," p.3; B. H. Carroll, Jr., *History of Houston,* p.200.

69. Deed Records of Austin County (County Clerk's office, Bellville), B, 33-34.

70. Deed Records of Harris County, D, 439-440.

71. B. H. Carroll, Jr., *History of Houston,* pp.327-328.

72. T. R. Fehrenbach, *History of Texas,* p.321.

73. Ibid.

74. Deed Records of Harris County, F, 398-9.

75. Deed Records of Harris County, G, 347-8.

76. Andrew Forest Muir, "William Marsh Rice, His Life and Death," p.5.

77. T. R. Fehrenbach, *History of Texas,* p.261.

78. Ibid.; Andrew Forest Muir, "William Marsh Rice, Houstonian," *East Texas Historical Journal,* II, 1, p.34.

79. M. Johnston, *Happy Worldly Abode,* p.54.

80. William Marsh Rice to "Friend Marks," April 24, 1900 (Rice Litigation Papers, Fondren Library).

81. S. B. Southwick, *Galveston Old and New* (Galveston, no date), p.347.

82. Texas Treasury Papers, Vol. III, 1038-1039 (No. 1656) and 1049-1050 (No. 1671) (Texas State Library, Austin, Texas).

83. Houston *Morning Star,* December 24, 1844.

84. Harris Masterson Papers, Fondren Library, Rice University, Houston, Texas.

85. B. H. Carroll, Jr., *History of Houston,* p.75.

86. Houston *Telegraph and Texas Register,* August 4, 1841, p.2, col. 5 and p.3, col. 1.

87. B. H. Carroll, Jr., *History of Houston,* p.75.

88. Ibid, p.342.

89. Ibid., p.343.

90. William Marsh Rice to W. G. Rucker, May 6, 1900 (William Marsh Rice Papers, Fondren Library).

91. B. H. Carroll, Jr., *History of Houston,* p.81.

92. Ibid., p.226.

93. Andrew Forest Muir, "William Marsh Rice, His Life and Death," p.3.

94. Ibid., p.9.

95. Robert S. Maxwell, *Whistle in the Piney Woods: Paul Bremond and the Houston, East and West Texas Railway* (Houston, Texas, Texas Gulf Coast Historical Association, November, 1963), VII, 2, p.4.

96. Ibid., p.5.

97. Ibid.

98. Ibid., p.7.

99. Andrew Forest Muir, "William Marsh Rice, His Life and Death," p.8.

100. B. H. Carroll, Jr., *History of Houston,* p.238.

101. R. S. Maxwell, *Paul Bremond,* p.7.

102. Andrew Forest Muir, "William Marsh Rice, His Life and Death," p.8.

103. Ibid., p.3.

104. S. O. Young, *True Stories of Old Houston and Houstonians* (Galveston: Oscar Springer, 1913), p.39.

105. Asbury First Methodist Church Register (Springfield, Massachusetts), 1815-1838; *New York Times,* January 15, 1901.

106. *New York Times,* January 15, 1901; Frank McKee to Edgar Odell Lovett, "The Family of William Marsh Rice" (Lovett Papers, Fondren Library).

107. S. O. Young, *Old Houston and Houstonians,* p.38.

108. O. P. Allen, "The Late William Marsh Rice."

109. Andrew Forest Muir manuscript, p.6 (Andrew Forest Muir Papers, Fondren Library).

110. Charlotte McKee to William Marsh Rice, October 19, 1898 (Rice Litigation Papers, Fondren Library).

111. Frank McKee to Edgar Odell Lovett, "The Family of William Marsh Rice" (Lovett Papers, Fondren Library); O. P. Allen, "The Late William Marsh Rice."

112. Andrew Forest Muir, "William Marsh Rice and His Institute," p.2.

113. M. Johnston, *Happy Worldly Abode,* p.68.

114. Marriage Records of Harris County, Vol. B, p.255; *Democratic Telegram and Texas Register,* July 4, 1850, p.3, col. 4.

115. Andrew Forest Muir to Mrs. Bremond, June 29, 1957 (Muir Papers, Fondren Library); Andrew Forest Muir, "William Marsh Rice, His Life and Death," p.13.

116. Minerva Rice Olds to William Marsh Rice, March 16, 1899 (Rice Litigation Papers, Fondren Library).

117. 1850 Census, Schedule 1, Texas (National Archives, Washington, D. C.), Harris County, p.8.

118. Writers' Program, *Houston, A History and Guide* (Houston: The Anson Jones Press, 1942), p.321.

119. Ibid., pp.320-321.

120. Ibid.

121. B. H. Carroll, Jr., *History of Houston,* p.64.

122. Ibid., p.69.

123. Ibid., p.430.

124. Ibid., pp.430-431.

125. M. Johnston, *Happy Worldly Abode,* p.64.

126. R. S. Maxwell, *Paul Bremond,* p.7.

127. Christ Church Subscription List for 1848, Christ Church Cathedral, Houston, Texas.

128. M. Johnston, *Happy Worldly Abode,* p.59; Christ Church Records, no date.

129. Christ Church Rectory Subscription, March 16, 1858, Christ Church Cathedral, Houston, Texas.

130. M. Johnston, *Happy Worldly Abode,* p.67.

131. Ibid., p.97.

132. Ibid., p.55.

133. Andrew Forest Muir, "William Marsh Rice, His Life and Death," p.16; Deed Records of Harris County, March 9, 1857.

134. Andrew Forest Muir, "The Beginnings of the Rice Institute," p.11 (Muir Papers, Fondren Library).

135. Andrew Forest Muir, "William Marsh Rice, His Life and Death," p.15.

136. *Texas Treasury Papers,* III, 1132 (No. 1788).

137. Andrew Forest Muir, "William Marsh Rice, His Life and Death," p.15.

138. Andrew Forest Muir, "William Marsh Rice, Houstonian," p.34.

139. Charles D. Green, *Fire Fighters of Houston, 1838-1915* (Houston: no publisher, 1915), p.19.

140. Andrew Forest Muir, "William Marsh Rice, His Life and Death," p.14.

141. Wille Hutcheson, "Houston's Old Homesteads," Houston *Post* between 1911 and 1914 (Alice C. Dean Notebooks, Fondren Library, Rice University, Houston, Texas).

142. Andrew Forest Muir, "William Marsh Rice, His Life and Death," p.6.

143. Deed Records of Brazoria County (MS in County Clerk's office, Angleton), E, 119-121.

144. *Richardson's Galveston Directory for 1859-1860* (Galveston: News Office, 1859); Charles W. Hayes, *Island and City of Galveston, 1876* (typescript in Rosenberg Library Archives, Galveston, Texas).

145. Minnie Rice Lummis to William Marsh Rice, January 1, 1899 (Rice Litigation Papers, Fondren Library).

146. Andrew Forest Muir, "William Marsh Rice, His Life and Death," p.12.

147. *Weekly Telegraph,* August 12, 1858.

148. T. R. Fehrenbach, *History of Texas,* p.321.

149. Deed Records of Harris County, S, 204-255.

150. Ibid., V, 452-453.

151. Ibid., X, 78-81.

152. "Centennial Souvenir of the New England Conference," p.17.

153. T. R. Fehrenbach, *History of Texas,* pp.205-206.

154. U. S. Census of 1860, Texas, Schedule 2, Harris County, p.23.

155. Deed Records of Montgomery County (County Clerk's office, Conroe), M, 165-167.

156. Deed Records of Harris County, Z, 522.

157. *Democratic Telegraph and Texas Register,* March 14, 1851, p.2, col. 4 and March 21, 1851, p.2, col. 4.

158. Deed Records of Harris County, N, 53-54.

159. T. R. Fehrenbach, *History of Texas,* pp.345-349.

160. Testimony of William A. Rice, of Wilbraham, Hampden County, March 26, 1904, at Springfield, Massachusetts (Rice Litigation Papers, Fondren Library).

161. Ibid.; *War of the Rebellion: Official Records of the Union and Confederate Armies* (Washington: Government Printing Office, 1901), 2.1, XXVIII, pt.2, 409.

162. Andrew Forest Muir, "William Marsh Rice, His Life and Death," p.17.

163. T. R. Fehrenbach, *History of Texas,* p.359.

164. Ibid., p.359.

165. *Tri-Weekly Telegraph,* December 20, 1861, 2 *e.*

166. T. R. Fehrenbach, *History of Texas,* p.369.

167. B. H. Carroll, Jr., *History of Houston,* p.454.

168. *Tri-Weekly Telegraph,* April 28, 1862, 1 *b.*

169. Ibid., June 6, 1862, 3 *d* and June 27, 1862, 2 *d.*

170. Ibid., October 29, 1862, 2 *b.*

171. Ibid., December 26, 1862, 2 *b.*

172. Ibid., December 31, 1862, 2 *b.*

173. *The War of the Rebellion: Official Records of the Union and Confederate Armies,* s. 1, XXXI, pt. 1, 740.

174. M. Johnston, *Happy Worldly Abode,* p.95.

175. Houston *Telegraph,* August 22, 1863.

176. Testimony of Mary Emma Todd, October 19, 1899 (Rice Litigation Papers, Fondren Library).

177. William McCraven, "To all whom it may concern," May 6, 1867 (William Marsh Rice Papers, Fondren Library).

178. T. R. Fehrenbach, *History of Texas,* p.371.

179. Handwritten, undated statement of William Marsh Rice (William Marsh Rice Papers, Fondren Library).

180. Will of William Marsh Rice, December 8, 1863 (William Marsh Rice Papers, Fondren Library).

181. Receipt signed Frank T. L'Estrange, July 17, 1865 (William Marsh Rice Papers, Fondren Library).

182. Handwritten, undated draft of statement by William Marsh Rice (William Marsh Rice Papers, Fondren Library).

183. Judith Anne Fenner, "Confederate Finances Abroad," unpublished Ph.D. thesis, Rice University, 1969.

184. T. R. Fehrenbach, *History of Texas,* p.359.

185. Tom Lea, *The King Ranch* (Boston: Little, Brown, 1957), pp.185-186.

186. T. R. Fehrenbach, *History of Texas,* p.388.

187. *Daily Telegraph,* April 4, 1864, 1 *b.*

188. Minutes of the Houston City Council, B, 95, City Secretary's Office, Houston.

189. "Re Mr. Clark's trip to Springfield, Mass., February 19-20, 1904" (Rice Litigation Papers, Fondren Library); Testimony of William Marsh Rice, March 26, 1904 (Rice Litigation Papers, Fondren Library).

190. Ibid.

191. Ibid.

192. Ibid.

193. H. P. N. Gammel, *The Laws of Texas 1822-1897* . . . (Austin: The Gammel Book Company, 1898), V, 1649-52.

194. Ibid., V, 1334-37.

195. Ibid., 116-119.

196. Andrew Forest Muir, "William Marsh Rice, His Life and Death," p.21.

197. Testimony of Charlotte S. McKee, March 31 and April 6, 1904 (Rice Litigation Papers, Fondren Library).

198. Ibid.

199. Will of William Marsh Rice dated June 18, 1867 (William Marsh Rice Papers, Fondren Library).

200. O. P. Allen, "The Late William Marsh Rice."

201. William Marsh Rice to Charlotte Rice McKee, March 23, 1899 (William Marsh Rice Papers, Fondren Library).

202. Natalie Clark, comp., J. H. Clark, "The Streets of Springfield with Biographical Notes and Clippings," typescript in the City Library of Springfield, Springfield, Massachusetts (1947), Vol. I, p.49.

203. Ibid.

204. Handwritten statement of William Marsh Rice, no date (Rice Litigation Papers, Fondren Library); M. Johnston, *Happy Worldly Abode,* p.98.

205. M. Johnston, *Happy Worldly Abode,* p.98.

206. Handwritten statement of William Marsh Rice, no date (Rice Litigation Papers, Fondren Library).

207. Andrew Forest Muir, "William Marsh Rice, His Life and Death," p.22.

208. C. C. Baldwin, *The Baldwin Family from 1500 to 1881* (Cleveland: no publisher, 1881), II, 1235-36.

209. Andrew Forest Muir, "The Second Mrs. Rice" (MS in Muir Papers, Fondren Library).

210. C. C. Baldwin, *Baldwin Family,* pp.1235-36.

211. Handwritten draft of a letter, undated, from William Marsh Rice to James Baker, Jr. (William Marsh Rice Papers, Fondren Library).

212. Handwritten agreement June 15, 1866 (William Marsh Rice Papers, Fondren Library).

213. Deed Records of Harris County, V, 594-595.

214. Handwritten statement by William Marsh Rice, undated (William Marsh Rice Papers, Fondren Library), p.2.

215. James A. Baker, Jr., "Reminiscences of the Founder," *The Rice Institute Pamphlet,* Vol. XVIII, No. 3 (July, 1931), p.135.

216. Andrew Forest Muir, "William Marsh Rice, His Life and Death," p.23.

217. Statement of William Marsh Rice (Rice Litigation Papers, Fondren Library), p.1.

218. Statement of William A. Rice, Springfield, Massachusetts, February 19-20, 1904 (Rice Litigation Papers, Fondren Library).

219. George E. Walton, *The Mineral Springs of the U.S. and Canada* (New York: D. Appleton & Co., 1874), pp.204 and 217.

220. Statement of William Marsh Rice (Rice Litigation Papers, Fondren Library).

221. Ibid.

222. Testimony of E. Raphael, Houston, Dec. 7, 1899 (Rice Litigation Papers, Fondren Library.)

223. William Marsh Rice to James A. Baker, Jr., September 26, 1896 (William Marsh Rice Papers, Fondren Library).

224. Robert S. Maxwell, *Paul Bremond,* p.7.

225. Testimony of Mary E. House, New York, October 10, 1899 (Rice Litigation Papers, Fondren Library).

226. William Marsh Rice to Mrs. Groesbeeck, March, 1899 (William Marsh Rice Papers, Fondren Library).

227. Statement of William Marsh Rice (Rice Litigation Papers, Fondren Library).

228. Ibid.

229. Ibid.

230. Statement of James A. Baker, Jr. (Rice Litigation Papers, Fondren Library).

231. Statement of William Marsh Rice (Rice Litigation Papers, Fondren Library).

232. Testimony of Charlotte Rice McKee, Springfield, Massachusetts, March 31 and April 6, 1904 (Rice Litigation Papers, Fondren Library).

233. Register of Births, Marriages and Deaths in the Town of Belchertown, Commonwealth of Massachusetts, Vol. A, pp.56-57.

234. Central Railroad of New Jersey and Branches, *Travellers and Tourists Guide* (New York: American Bank Note Company, ca. 1880), p.8.

235. Deed Records of Somerset County, New Jersey (MS in County Clerk's Office, Somerville), I-4, 600-603 and F-2, 626-629.

236. Testimony of Charlotte Rice McKee, Springfield, Massachusetts, March 31 and April 6, 1904 (Rice Litigation Papers, Fondren Library).

237. Surrogate Case Papers of Somerset County, New Jersey, File 7608 (Collins McKee, dec'd).

238. George A. Trust in a conversation with Andrew Forest Muir, January 3, 1958 (Muir Papers, Fondren Library).

239. Testimony of Josephine Trust, October 24, 1899 (Rice Litigation Papers, Fondren Library); Testimony of Charlotte Rice McKee, March 31 and April 6, 1904 (Rice Litigation Papers, Fondren Library).

240. Springfield *Daily Republican*, March 29, 1872, p.3, col.2.

241. Testimony of Charlotte Rice McKee, March 31 and April 6, 1904 (Rice Litigation Papers, Fondren Library).

242. Ibid.

243. Testimony of Conrad Cramer, New York, October 22, 1899 (Rice Litigation Papers, Fondren Library).

244. Testimony of Charlotte Rice McKee, March 31 and April 6, 1904 (Rice Litigation Papers, Fondren Library).

245. Testimony of Mary Emma Todd, New York, October 19, 1899 (Rice Litigation Papers, Fondren Library).

246. Deed Records of Somerset County, K-5, 464-468 and 416-421.

247. Testimony of Blanchard Fosgate, New York, October 30, 1899 (Rice Litigation Papers, Fondren Library).

248. Testimony of Paul Reusch, New York, October 26, 1899 (Rice Litigation Papers, Fondren Library).

249. Testimony of Blanchard Fosgate, New York, October 30, 1899 (Rice Litigation Papers, Fondren Library).

250. Ibid. and exhibits 1-5 attached to original deposition.

251. George A. Trust in a conversation with Andrew Forest Muir, January 3, 1958 (Muir Papers, Fondren Library).

252. Testimony of Charlotte Rice McKee, March 31 and April 6, 1904 (Rice Litigation Papers, Fondren Library).

253. Testimony of Furman H. Gise, New York, October 25, 1899 (Rice Litigation Papers, Fondren Library).

254. William Marsh Rice to Arthur B. Cohn, September, 1899 (William Marsh Rice Papers, Fondren Library).

255. Testimony of Blanchard Fosgate, New York, October 30, 1899 (Rice Litigation Papers, Fondren Library).

256. Testimony of Furman H. Gise, New York, October 25, 1899 (Rice Litigation Papers, Fondren Library).

257. Testimony of John Cooper, New York, October 25, 1899 (Rice Litigation Papers, Fondren Library).

258. "Pullman Palace Drawing-Room and Sleeping Cars Run Through From Texas to St. Louis Without Change, And With But One Change To New York and Other Large Cities in the East" (Wrapper Title) (Boston: Rand, Avey & Co., no date) (Andrew Forest Muir Papers, Fondren Library).

259. Testimony of Furman H. Gise, New York, October 25, 1899 (Rice Litigation Papers, Fondren Library).

260. Testimony of Paul Reusch, New York, October 26, 1899 (Rice Litigation Papers, Fondren Library).

261. Ibid.

262. Testimony of Conrad Cramer, New York, October 22, 1899 (Rice Litigation Papers, Fondren Library).

263. Testimony of Paul Reusch, New York, October 26, 1899 (Rice Litigation Papers, Fondren Library).

264. Testimony of Furman H. Gise, New York, October 26, 1899 (Rice Litigation Papers, Fondren Library).

265. Testimony of George Fisher, New York, October 26, 1899 (Rice Litigation Papers, Fondren Library).

266. Testimony of Josephine Trust, New York, October 24, 1899 (Rice Litigation Papers, Fondren Library).

267. Ibid.; Testimony of Lizzie M. Lages, October 25, 1899 and Katie G. Trust, October 24, 1899 (Rice Litigation Papers, Fondren Library).

268. Testimony of Isabel H. Carpenter, New York, November 2, 1899 (Rice Litigation Papers, Fondren Library).

269. Ibid.

270. Testimony of Charles Carpenter, New York, October 22, 1899 (Rice Litigation Papers, Fondren Library).

271. Testimony of Conrad Cramer, New York, October 22, 1899 (Rice Litigation Papers, Fondren Library).

272. William Marsh Rice to Michael Caton, March 5, 1882 (William Marsh Rice Papers, Fondren Library).

273. William Marsh Rice to James A. Baker, Jr., New York, September

26, 1896 (Rice Litigation Papers, Fondren Library).

274. W. B. Botts and others to William Marsh Rice, January 3, 1879 (William Marsh Rice Papers, Fondren Library).

275. Testimony of Emanuel Raphael, Houston, December 7, 1899 (Rice Litigation Papers, Fondren Library).

276. Ibid.

277. Andrew Forest Muir, "The Beginnings of the Rice Institute" (Muir Papers, Fondren Library), p.11.

278. Interview with Ruth Gillette Hardy, January 6, 1958 (Andrew Forest Muir Papers, Fondren Library).

279. Henry W. Arey, *The Girard College and Its Founder* (Philadelphia: C. Sherman, 1854), p.20.

280. Ibid., pp.25 and 38.

281. Allan Nevins, *Abram S. Hewitt, With Some Account of Peter Cooper* (New York: Harper & Brothers, 1935), pp.77 and 115.

282. Cesar Lombardi to his grandchildren, October 31, 1915 (Muir Papers, Fondren Library).

283. Testimony of John D. Bartine, New York, November 3, 1899 (Rice Litigation Papers, Fondren Library).

284. New York *Sun,* October 12, 1900.

285. H. W. Arey, *Girard College,* p.74.

286. A. Nevins, *Abram S. Hewitt,* p.176.

287. Testimony of John D. Bartine, New York, November 3, 1899 (Rice Litigation Papers, Fondren Library); Will of William Marsh Rice, January 28, 1882 (William Marsh Rice Papers, Fondren Library).

288. Ibid.

289. Ibid.

290. H. W. Arey, *Girard College,* p.73.

291. Will of William Marsh Rice, January 28, 1882 (William Marsh Rice Papers, Fondren Library).

292. Testimony of Emanuel Raphael, Houston, December 7, 1899 (Rice Litigation Papers, Fondren Library).

293. Testimony of George F. Brown, New York, October 3, 1899 (Rice Litigation Papers, Fondren Library).

294. Testimony of George N. Fisher, New York, October 26, 1899 (Rice Litigation Papers, Fondren Library).

295. Testimony of Mary E. House, New York, October 10, 1899 (Rice Litigation Papers, Fondren Library).

296. Testimony of Lilla McDougall Boothby, New York, October 18, 1899 (Rice Litigation Papers, Fondren Library).

297. Testimony of Isabel H. Carpenter, New York, November 2, 1899 (Rice Litigation Papers, Fondren Library).

298. Testimony of Mary E. House, New York, October 10, 1899 (Rice Litigation Papers, Fondren Library).

299. Testimony of Laura Geddes Morton, New York, September 23, 1899 (Rice Litigation Papers, Fondren Library).

300. Elizabeth Baldwin Rice to Josephine Trust, March 5, 1882 (William Marsh Rice Papers, Fondren Library).

301. William Marsh Rice to James A. Baker, Jr., September 26, 1896 (Hornblower, Byrne, Miller & Potter, *Brief for Respondent* [New York: C. G. Burgoyne, 1903], pp.65-66, citing transcript of proceedings in Surrogate's Court, folios 2354-58).

302. Testimony of Mary E. Todd, New York, October 19, 1899 (Rice Litigation Papers, Fondren Library).

303. Testimony of Alice H. Adams, New York, October 31, 1899 (Rice Litigation Papers, Fondren Library).

304. Testimony of Laura Geddes Morton, New York, September 23, 1899 (Rice Litigation Papers, Fondren Library).

305. Ibid.

306. Deed Records of Brazoria County (MS in County Clerk's Office, Angleton, Texas), E, 115-119.

307. Testimony of Alice H. Adams, New York, October 31, 1899 (Rice Litigation Papers, Fondren Library).

308. Testimony of Laura Baldwin Morton, New York, September 22, 1899 (Rice Litigation Papers, Fondren Library).

309. Ibid.

310. Testimony of Josephine Trust, New York, October 24, 1899 (Rice Litigation Papers, Fondren Library).

311. Testimony of Lizzie M. Lages, New York, October 25, 1899 (Rice Litigation Papers, Fondren Library).

312. Testimony of Sarah J. Lippincott, New York, November 6, 1899 (Rice Litigation Papers, Fondren Library).

313. Testimony of Elizabeth S. Glassford, New York, October 3, 1899 (Rice Litigation Papers, Fondren Library).

314. Testimony of Sarah J. Lippincott, New York, November 6, 1899 (Rice Litigation Papers, Fondren Library).

315. Testimony of Maria Van Alstyne, New York, October 17, 1899 (Rice Litigation Papers, Fondren Library).

316. Testimony of Alice H. Adams, New York, October 31, 1899 (Rice Litigation Papers, Fondren Library).

317. Testimony of Nadine Neftel, New York, October 16, 1899 (Rice Litigation Papers, Fondren Library).

318. *The Drawing Room Sixth Annual Report of the Executive Committee,* 1890 (New York: no publisher, no date), p.8.

319. *Twelfth Annual Report of the New York Diet Kitchen Association for*

Providing Nourishing Food for the Sick Poor for the Year Ending December 31, 1884 (New York: Martin B. Brown, Printer and Stationer, 1882), p.3.

320. *Ninth Annual Report of the New York Diet Kitchen . . . for the Year Ending December 31, 1881* (New York: Martin B. Brown, Printer and Stationer, 1882), p.8.

321. M. Johnston, *Happy Worldly Abode*, p.12.

322. Houston Daily *Post* of April 8, 1881, quoted in Writers' Program, *Houston, A History and Guide*, p.254.

323. Ibid., pp.253-254.

324. Deed Records of Harris County, Vol. 32, pp.98-102.

325. Mortgage Records of Harris County, March 12, 1886, Vol. 13.

326. Charters of Incorporation (MS in Secretary of State's Office Austin, Texas), File 4043, April 11, 1889.

327. Walter Prescott Webb, ed., *The Handbook of Texas* (Austin: The Texas State Historical Association, 1952), II, 74, col. 2.

328. Autobiographical Letters of Cesar Lombardi to his grandchildren (Muir Papers, Fondren Library), p.3. Lombardi has apparently confused General James Samuel Wadsworth (1807-1864) with his father, James Wadsworth (1768-1844), who built and endowed the Geneseo library.

329. Ibid., p.73.

330. Ibid., p.74.

331. Ibid.

332. Ibid., p.74-75.

333. S. O. Young, *Old Houston and Houstonians*, p.116.

334. J. T. McCants, "Some Information Concerning the Rice Institute," MS in the Fondren Library, Rice University, p.82.

335. Testimony of Emanuel Raphael, Houston, December 7, 1899 (Rice Litigation Papers, Fondren Library).

336. Ibid.; J. T. McCants, "Rice Institute," p.83.

337. Deed of Indenture of May 16, 1891, Harris County, Texas (in J. T. McCants, "Rice Institute," p.97).

338. Ibid.

339. Ibid.

340. Testimony of Emanuel Raphael, Houston, December 7, 1899 (Rice Litigation Papers, Fondren Library).

341. Testimony of Conrad Cramer, New York, October 22, 1899 and testimony of Lizzie M. Lages, New York, October 25, 1899 (Rice Litigation Papers, Fondren Library).

342. Testimony of Emanuel Raphael, Houston, December 7, 1899 (Rice Litigation Papers, Fondren Library).

343. Deed Records of Somerset County, New Jersey, Y-6, 367-371.

344. Testimony of Emanuel Raphael, Houston, December 7, 1899 (Rice

Litigation Papers, Fondren Library).

345. Testimony of Maria Van Alstyne, New York, October 17, 1899 (Rice Litigation Papers, Fondren Library).

346. Testimony of Sarah J. Lippincott, New York, November 6, 1899 (Rice Litigation Papers, Fondren Library).

347. Last Will and Testament of Elizabeth Baldwin Rice, January 27, 1892, annexed to the testimony of Ruth A. Watrous, New York, October 13, 1899 (Rice Litigation Papers, Fondren Library).

348. Testimony of Emanuel Raphael, Houston, December 7, 1890 (Rice Litigation Papers, Fondren Library).

349. Ibid.

350. Ibid.

351. J. T. McCants, "Rice Institute," p.16.

352. Testimony of Emanuel Raphael, Houston, December 7, 1899 (Rice Litigation Papers, Fondren Library).

353. Ibid.

354. James Everett McAshan to James A. Baker, Jr., January 15, 1901 (William Marsh Rice Papers, Fondren Library).

355. J. J. Pastoriza to Baker, Botts, Baker and Lovett, Houston, November 16, 1900 (William Marsh Rice Papers, Fondren Library).

356. Testimony of Emanuel Raphael, Houston, December 7, 1899 (Rice Litigation Papers, Fondren Library).

357. Bills of the Capitol Hotel, December 1893 to November 1894 (William Marsh Rice Papers, Fondren Library).

358. Testimony of Emanuel Raphael, Houston, December 7, 1899 (Rice Litigation Papers, Fondren Library).

359. Ibid., and William Marsh Rice to Arthur B. Cohn, August 30, 1898 (Estate of William Marsh Rice, Fondren Library).

360. Testimony of Emanuel Raphael, Houston, December 7, 1899 (Rice Litigation Papers, Fondren Library).

361. Testimony of Mary E. House, New York, October 10, 1899 (Rice Litigation Papers, Fondren Library).

362. Testimony of Jenny Wilson Rushmore, Houston, February 7, 1900 (Rice Litigation Papers, Fondren Library).

363. Testimony of Alice H. Adams, New York, October 31, 1899 (Rice Litigation Papers, Fondren Library).

364. Testimony of John Edward Matheson, New York, October 22, 1899 (Rice Litigation Papers, Fondren Library).

365. William Marsh Rice to Arthur B. Cohn, August 30, 1898 (William Marsh Rice Papers, Fondren Library).

366. Testimony of Hannah C. Morris, New York, November 1, 1899 (Rice Litigation Papers, Fondren Library).

367. Andrew Forest Muir, "William Marsh Rice and His Institute," p.9.

368. Galveston *Daily News,* May 24, 1895, p.2, col. 6.

369. Testimony of Elizabeth S. Glassford, New York, October 3, 1899 (Rice Litigation Papers, Fondren Library).

370. Testimony of Laura Baldwin Morton, New York, September 22, 1899 (Rice Litigation Papers, Fondren Library).

371. Testimony of Mary E. Todd, New York, October 19, 1899 (Rice Litigation Papers, Fondren Library).

372. Testimony of Hannah C. Morris, New York, November 1, 1899 (Rice Litigation Papers, Fondren Library).

373. Testimony of Jenny Wilson Rushmore, Houston, February 7, 1900 (Rice Litigation Papers, Fondren Library).

374. Testimony of Laura Baldwin Morton, New York, October 4, 1899 (Rice Litigation Papers, Fondren Library).

375. Testimony of John E. Matheson, New York, October 22, 1899 (Rice Litigation Papers, Fondren Library).

376. Handwritten statement by William Marsh Rice in the files of Hornblower, Byrne, Miller and Potter, no date (William Marsh Rice Papers, Fondren Library).

377. William Marsh Rice to W. S. Campbell, January 6, 1900 (Rice Litigation Papers, Fondren Library).

378. William Marsh Rice to W. S. Campbell, January 3, 1900 (Rice Litigation Papers, Fondren Library).

379. William Marsh Rice to W. S. Campbell, January 4, 1899 (William Marsh Rice Papers, Fondren Library).

380. Ibid.

381. Last Will and Testament of Elizabeth Baldwin Rice, Houston, June 1, 1896 (Rice Litigation Papers, Fondren Library).

382. Andrew Forest Muir, "William Marsh Rice and His Institute," p.9.

383. Last Will and Testament of Elizabeth Baldwin Rice, June 1, 1896 (Rice Litigation Papers, Fondren Library).

384. Ibid.

385. William Marsh Rice to Laura Geddes Morton, July 21, 1896 (Rice Litigation Papers, Fondren Library).

386. Handwritten statement by William Marsh Rice in the files of Hornblower, Byrne, Miller and Potter, no date (William Marsh Rice Papers, Fondren Library).

387. William Marsh Rice to Laura Geddes Morton, July 21, 1896 (Rice Litigation Papers, Fondren Library).

388. Katherine Schoefle to Marie Le Duc, August 8, 1896 (William Marsh Rice Papers, Fondren Library) and testimony of Emanuel Raphael, Houston, December 7, 1899 (Rice Litigation Papers, Fondren Library).

389. William Marsh Rice to Laura Geddes Morton, July 29, 1896 (Rice

Litigation Papers, Fondren Library).

390. Katherine Schoefle to Marie Le Duc, August 8, 1896 (William Marsh Rice Papers, Fondren Library).

391. William Marsh Rice to William S. Campbell, January 3, 1900 (Rice Litigation Papers, Fondren Library).

392. William Marsh Rice to Laura Geddes Morton, August 4, 1896 (Rice Litigation Papers, Fondren Library).

393. Testimony of Mary E. Turnure, New York, September 25, 1899 (Rice Litigation Papers, Fondren Library).

394. Andrew Forest Muir, "William Marsh Rice and His Institute," p.10.

395. Last Will and Testament of Elizabeth Baldwin Rice, June 1, 1896 (Rice Litigation Papers, Fondren Library).

396. Handwritten memorandum in the files of Hornblower, Byrne, Miller and Potter, no date (William Marsh Rice Papers, Fondren Library).

397. Andrew Forest Muir, "William Marsh Rice and His Institute," p.10.

398. Andrew Forest Muir, "William Marsh Rice, His Life and Death," p.33.

399. Andrew Forest Muir, "William Marsh Rice and His Institute," p.10.

400. Statement of Charles F. Jones, no date (Andrew Forest Muir Papers, Fondren Library).

401. Ibid.

402. Ibid.

403. New York *World,* September 27, 1900.

404. William Marsh Rice to P. M. Granberry, January 20, 1899 (William Marsh Rice Papers, Fondren Library).

405. Statement of Charles F. Jones (Muir Papers, Fondren Library).

406. William Marsh Rice to Arthur B. Cohn, March 10, 1898 (William Marsh Rice Papers, Fondren Library).

407. Statement of Charles F. Jones (Muir Papers, Fondren Library).

408. New York *Journal,* September 27, 1900.

409. William Marsh Rice to Arthur B. Cohn, July 7, 1895 (William Marsh Rice Papers, Fondren Library).

410. William Marsh Rice to Mary C. Brewster, March 27, 1898 (William Marsh Rice Papers, Fondren Library).

411. William Marsh Rice to Arthur B. Cohn, January 24, 1898 (William Marsh Rice Papers, Fondren Library).

412. William Marsh Rice to Charlotte Rice McKee, March 23, 1899 (William Marsh Rice Papers, Fondren Library).

413. Testimony of Arthur B. Cohn, Court of Appeals, State of New York: *The People of the State of New York, Respondents, against Albert T. Patrick, Appellant* (New York: W. P. Mitchell and Sons, Printers, [1905]), I. 505. Hereafter referred to as Court of Appeals, State of New York (Mitchell).

414. William Marsh Rice to Arthur B. Cohn, September 24, 1895 (William Marsh Rice Papers, Fondren Library).

415. Arthur B. Cohn to William Marsh Rice, April 29, 1899 (William Marsh Rice Papers, Fondren Library).

416. William Marsh Rice to Arthur B. Cohn, April 15, 1899 (William Marsh Rice Papers, Fondren Library).

417. William Marsh Rice to Arthur B. Cohn, February 7, 1900 (William Marsh Rice Papers, Fondren Library).

418. William Marsh Rice to Arthur B. Cohn, December 7, 1898 (William Marsh Rice Papers, Fondren Library).

419. William Marsh Rice to Arthur B. Cohn, November 30, 1898 (William Marsh Rice Papers, Fondren Library).

420. Best and Russell Company, of Havana, to William Marsh Rice, 1897 (William Marsh Rice Papers, Fondren Library).

421. William Marsh Rice to Arthur B. Cohn, January 26, 1899 (William Marsh Rice Papers, Fondren Library).

422. Mary Louise Bremond to William Marsh Rice, undated, copy (Rice Litigation Papers, Fondren Library).

423. Statement of Mrs. A. S. Capron, New York City, October 24, 1900 (Rice Litigation Papers, Fondren Library).

424. Arthur B. Cohn to William Marsh Rice, July 7, 1896 (William Marsh Rice Papers, Fondren Library).

425. Arthur B. Cohn to William Marsh Rice, December 12, 1897 (William Marsh Rice Papers, Fondren Library).

426. Arthur B. Cohn to William Marsh Rice, August 3, 1898 (William Marsh Rice Papers, Fondren Library).

427. Testimony of Laura Baldwin Morton, September 22, 1899 (Rice Litigation Papers, Fondren Library).

428. Testimony of Maria Van Alstyne, New York, October 17, 1899 (Rice Litigation Papers, Fondren Library).

429. M. Johnston, *Happy Worldly Abode,* p.67.

430. Malvina Warham Brewster, "Mrs. Mary C. Brewster," *Confederate Veteran* (May, 1906), XIV.

431. William Marsh Rice to Mary C. Brewster, January 8, 1899 (William Marsh Rice Papers, Fondren Library).

432. Mary C. Brewster to William Marsh Rice, July 31, 1898 (William Marsh Rice Papers, Fondren Library).

433. William Marsh Rice to Mary C. Brewster, June 27, 1897 (William Marsh Rice Papers, Fondren Library).

434. William Marsh Rice to Mary C. Brewster, September 23, 1898 (William Marsh Rice Papers, Fondren Library).

435. William Marsh Rice to Mary C. Brewster, October 26, 1897 (William Marsh Rice Papers, Fondren Library).

436. William Marsh Rice to Mary C. Brewster, November 1, 1898 (William Marsh Rice Papers, Fondren Library).

437. William Marsh Rice to Mary C. Brewster, August 4, 1898 (William Marsh Rice Papers, Fondren Library).

438. Memorandum of December 17, 1898, witnessing contract between O. T. Holt and A. T. Patrick (William Marsh Rice Papers, Fondren Library).

439. Biographical material on Albert T. Patrick, here and elsewhere, is taken from Andrew Forest Muir's paper presented before the Harris County Historical Society, September 6, 1955, "William Marsh Rice, His Life and Death, the History of a Fortune," unless otherwise noted (MS in Muir Papers, Fondren Library).

440. Testimony of Addie M. Francis, for people, before Magistrate Jerome, April 1, 1901—Record, IV, 3118 (Muir Papers, Fondren Library).

441. Testimony of Nadine Neftel, New York, October 16, 1899 and Testimony of Mary E. Todd, New York, October 19, 1899 (Rice Litigation Papers, Fondren Library).

442. Statement of Charles T. Adams, no date (William Marsh Rice Papers, Fondren Library). Testimony of Charles F. Jones, Court of Appeals, State of New York (Mitchell), II, 998 (William Marsh Rice Papers, Fondren Library).

443. New York *World,* October 6, 1900.

444. Court of Appeals, State of New York (Mitchell), II, 1163 (William Marsh Rice Papers, Fondren Library).

445. Ibid., II, 1003.

446. William Marsh Rice to Arthur B. Cohn, July 19, 1899 (William Marsh Rice Papers, Fondren Library).

447. William Marsh Rice to Root, April 21, 1899 (William Marsh Rice Papers, Fondren Library).

448. William Marsh Rice to Arthur B. Cohn, early 1899 (William Marsh Rice Papers, Fondren Library).

449. William Marsh Rice to James A. Baker, Jr., handwritten draft on back of letter from Arthur B. Cohn dated June 24, 1899 (William Marsh Rice Papers, Fondren Library).

450. Testimony of Paul Reusch, New York, October 26, 1899 (Rice Litigation Papers, Fondren Library).

451. Arthur B. Cohn to William M. Rice, October 29, 1897 (William Marsh Rice Papers, Fondren Library).

452. William Marsh Rice to Arthur B. Cohn, December 18, 1897 (William Marsh Rice Papers, Fondren Library).

453. William Marsh Rice to Arthur B. Cohn, April 30, 1899 (William Marsh Rice Papers, Fondren Library).

454. Testimony of Emanuel Raphael, Houston, December 7, 1899 (Rice Litigation Papers, Fondren Library).

455. Statement of Emanuel Raphael, undated, Hornblower, Byrne, Miller and Potter files (William Marsh Rice Papers, Fondren Library).

456. Emanuel Raphael to William Marsh Rice, November 4, 1897 (William Marsh Rice Papers, Fondren Library).

457. Statement of Emanuel Raphael, undated, Hornblower, Byrne, Miller and Potter files and Testimony of Emanuel Raphael, Houston, December 7, 1899 (William Marsh Rice Papers, Fondren Library).

458. Statement of Emanuel Raphael, undated, Hornblower, Byrne, Miller and Potter files (William Marsh Rice Papers, Fondren Library).

459. William Hayne Leavell to Hornblower, Byrne, Miller and Potter, June 5, 1901 (William Marsh Rice Papers, Fondren Library).

460. Charles Martin to William Marsh Rice, July 13, 1900 (William Marsh Rice Papers, Fondren Library).

461. William Marsh Rice, per Jones, to City Agent, U. S. Express Company, October 27, 1899 (William Marsh Rice Papers, Fondren Library).

462. "List of Books Shipped W. M. Rice, May 30, 1900" (William Marsh Rice Papers, Fondren Library).

463. William Marsh Rice to J. L. Blinn, 1899 (Rice Litigation Papers, Fondren Library).

464. *People v. Patrick*: Court of Appeals of New York, June 9, 1905, in *Northeastern Reporter* (St. Paul, Minnesota: West Publishing Company, 1885-1936), p.848 (hereafter referred to as *People v. Patrick [Northeastern Reporter]*). James A. Baker, Jr., "The Patrick Case," transcript of stenographic notes, privately printed August 6, 1954, p. 14.

465. Testimony of Walter O. Wetherbee, reported in New York *Evening Post*, October 18, 1900 (Muir Papers, Fondren Library).

466. Ibid.

467. Ibid.

468. Testimony of Walter O. Wetherbee, reported in New York *Commercial Advertiser*, October 18, 1900 (Muir Papers, Fondren Library).

469. Charles Carpenter in an interview with James A. Baker, Jr., October 4, 1900 (William Marsh Rice Papers, Fondren Library).

470. Charles Carpenter to James A. Baker, Jr., October 8, 1900 (William Marsh Rice Papers, Fondren Library).

471. *People v. Patrick (Northeastern Reporter)*, p.849.

472. New York *World*, October 6, 1900; Testimony of Walker Curry, M.D., Court of Appeals, State of New York (Mitchell), II, 1634.

473. J. J. Pastoriza to Baker, Botts, Baker and Lovett, November 16, 1900 (William Marsh Rice Papers, Fondren Library).

474. William Marsh Rice to Mary C. Brewster, May 19, 1900 (William Marsh Rice Papers, Fondren Library).

475. Maria Deane to William Marsh Rice, August 23, 1898 (William Marsh Rice Papers, Fondren Library).

476. *People v. Patrick (Northeastern Reporter)*, p.849.

477. James A. Baker, Jr., "The Patrick Case," p.15 (Muir Papers, Fondren Library); New York *Times,* March 19, 1902, p.10, col.3.

478. James A. Baker, Jr., "The Patrick Case," p.15.

479. Ibid., pp.15-16.

480. Testimony of Charles F. Jones, Court of Appeals, State of New York (Mitchell), II, p.1164.

481. New York *Times,* March 8, 1902, p.7, col.2.

482. Testimony of Walker Curry, M.D., Court of Appeals, State of New York (Mitchell), II, p.1649.

483. William Marsh Rice to Arthur B. Cohn, June 22, 1900 (William Marsh Rice Papers, Fondren Library).

484. Testimony of Charles F. Jones, Court of Appeals, State of New York (Mitchell), II, p.1124.

485. Ibid., II, p.1124; James A. Baker, Jr., Address of before Rice Institute Engineers' Society, November 13, 1929, p.27 (William Marsh Rice Papers, Fondren Library).

486. Testimony of William Lafayette Jones, Court of Appeals, State of New York (Mitchell), II, p.1376.

487. Testimony of Charles F. Jones, Court of Appeals, State of New York (Mitchell), II, p.1187.

488. James A. Baker, Jr., Address before the Rice Institute Engineers' Society, November 13, 1929, pp.16-17 (William Marsh Rice Papers, Fondren Library).

489. *People v. Patrick (Northeastern Reporter)*, p.852; Court of Appeals, State of New York (Mitchell), I, pp.915-920.

490. Court of Appeals, State of New York (Mitchell), II, p.1133.

491. M. Johnston, *Happy Worldly Abode,* p. 130.

492. Re *Rice:* Memorandum Concerning Merchants & Planters Oil Company Draft and Statement of B. B. Rice in reference to the drawing of drafts by the Merchants & Planters Oil Company on William M. Rice in September, 1900 (William Marsh Rice Papers, Fondren Library).

493. Henry Oliver to William Marsh Rice, September 11, 1900 (William Marsh Rice Papers, Fondren Library).

494. William Marsh Rice to Henry Oliver, September 15, 1900 (William Marsh Rice Papers, Fondren Library).

495. William Marsh Rice to James A. Baker, Jr., draft, September 1900 (William Marsh Rice Papers, Fondren Library).

496. Ibid.

497. Re *Rice:* Memorandum Concerning Merchants & Planters Oil Company Draft (William Marsh Rice Papers, Fondren Library).

498. New York *Herald,* September 26, 1900.

499. New York *Evening Herald,* November 2, 1900.

500. Court of Appeals, State of New York (Mitchell), II, p.1134.

501. New York *Herald,* October 29, 1900.

502. Court of Appeals, State of New York (Mitchell), II, pp.2002-08.

503. Ibid., II, p.1637.

504. *People v. Patrick (Northeastern Reporter),* p.849.

505. Ibid.

506. Court of Appeals, State of New York (Mitchell), II, p.1181.

507. Ibid., II, p.1143.

508. *People v. Patrick (Northeastern Reporter),* p.846.

509. Court of Appeals, State of New York (Mitchell), II, p.1143.

510. Ibid., II, p. 1145.

511. New York *Herald,* September 27, 1900.

512. Court of Appeals, State of New York (Mitchell), III, pp.2038-44.

513. Mrs. T. E. Thompson to James A. Baker, Jr., November 7, 1900 and Statement of Paul Teich, October 6, 1900 (William Marsh Rice Papers, Fondren Library).

514. Clark Bell, "The Medico-Legal Questions Arising in the Case of Patrick, Convicted of the Murder of Rice by Alleged Inhalation of Chloroform" (Library of Congress, RA1228 .M48, copyright March 11, 1905), pp.10-11.

515. Statement of Paul Teich, October 6, 1900 (William Marsh Rice Papers, Fondren Library).

516. Statement of Charles Plowright, October 26, 1900 (William Marsh Rice Papers, Fondren Library).

517. *People v. Patrick (Northeastern Reporter),* p.855.

518. Statement of John H. Wallace, September 24, 1900 (William Marsh Rice Papers, Fondren Library).

519. Charles F. Jones to James A. Baker, Jr., September 24, 1900 (William Marsh Rice Papers, Fondren Library).

520. James A. Baker, Jr., "The Patrick Case."

521. William Hayne Leavall to James A. Baker, Jr., October 8, 1900 (William Marsh Rice Papers, Fondren Library).

522. James A. Baker, Jr., "The Patrick Case," p.7.

523. Statement of James W. Gerard, undated (William Marsh Rice Papers, Fondren Library).

524. *People v. Patrick (Northeastern Reporter),* p.851.

525. Statement of R. A. Witthaus, New York *Sun,* October 28, 1900.

526. New York *Telegram,* September 27, 1900; New York *Evening World,* September 27, 1900.

527. New York *Evening Journal,* September 28, 1900.

528. James A. Baker, Jr., to R. S. Lovett, October 2, 1900 (William Marsh Rice Papers, Fondren Library).

529. R. Cornelius Raby, *Fifty Famous Trials* (Washington: Washington Law Book Co., 1937), pp.251-257.

530. *People v. Patrick (Northeastern Reporter),* p.850.

531. New York *Evening World,* October 5, 1900.

532. New York *Times,* October 19, 1900; Statement of E. Raphael, undated, Hornblower, Byrne, Miller and Potter files (William Marsh Rice Papers, Fondren Library).

533. New York *Sun,* October 28, 1900.

534. New York *Herald,* October 29, 1900.

535. New York *Times,* October 7, 1900.

536. New York *Evening Sun,* November 1, 1900.

537. New York *Evening Telegram,* November 2, 1900.

538. Court of Appeals, State of New York (Mitchell), V, p.4106.

539. New York *Sun,* January 14, 1901.

540. New York *Times,* January 15, 1901.

541. New York *Morning World,* May 26, 1901.

542. Andrew Forest Muir MS, no date, p.14 (Muir Papers, Fondren Library).

543. New York *Evening Telegram,* March 29, 1901.

544. Andrew Forest Muir MS, no date, p.14 (Muir Papers, Fondren Library).

545. Ibid., p.14.

546. New York *Evening Telegram,* April 23, 1901; New York *Morning World,* April 26, 1901.

547. *People v. Patrick (Northeastern Reporter),* p.858.

548. Ibid., p.845.

549. Andrew Forest Muir MS, no date, p.17 (Muir Papers, Fondren Library). *Time,* Nov., 1954.

550. New York *Morning Journal,* April 19, 1901.

551. New York *Morning World,* April 25, 1901.

552. New York *Times,* January 21, 1902, p.2, col. 6.

553. New York *Times,* January 23, 1902, p.1, col. 7.

554. New York *Times,* March 29, 1902, p.5, cols. 6-7.

555. New York *Times,* February 14, 1902, p.7, col. 2.

556. New York *Times,* March 25, 1902, p.7, col. 2.

557. New York *Times,* May 9, 1902, p.16, col. 1.

558. R. C. Raby, *Fifty Famous Trials,* p.255.

559. Clark Bell, "The Medico-Legal Questions," p.14.

560. R. C. Raby, *Fifty Famous Trials,* pp.255-256.

561. Andrew Forest Muir, "A Man Morbidly Virtuous—Albert T. Patrick" (MS in Muir Papers, Fondren Library), p.19.

562. Andrew Forest Muir, "The Beginnings of the Rice Institute" (MS in Muir Papers, Fondren Library), p.21.

563. Court of Appeals, State of New York, *Adele Baldwin and others v. William M. Rice, Jr., and others* (Court of Appeals, vol.2301, in New York Law Institute) [1], p.6.

564. Andrew Forest Muir, "The Beginnings of the Rice Institute," p.21.

565. J. T. McCants, "Rice Institute," p.13.

566. Ibid., p.16.

567. Julian Huxley, "Texas and Academe," *Cornhill Magazine,* CXVIII (July, 1918), p.53.

568. J. T. McCants, "Rice Institute," p.35.

569. J. Huxley, "Texas and Academe," p.59.

570. Ralph Adams Cram in *The Southern Architectural Review,* November, 1910, p.111, quoted in J. T. McCants, "Rice Institute," p.38.

571. J. Huxley, "Texas and Academe," p.59.

572. Ibid., pp.64-65.

573. Ibid., pp.55-56.

APPENDIX

1. CHARTER OF INCORPORATION OF THE WILLIAM M. RICE INSTITUTE FOR THE ADVANCEMENT OF LITERATURE, SCIENCE, AND ART (citing William Marsh Rice's Indenture of May 16, 1891), May 18, 1891.

2. ELIZABETH BALDWIN RICE'S CONTESTED WILL (June 1, 1896).

3. WILLIAM MARSH RICE'S WILL (under which the Rice Institute was the principal legatee), September 26, 1896.

4. THE FORGED OR PATRICK WILL, June 30, 1900.

CHARTER OF INCORPORATION OF THE WILLIAM M. RICE INSTITUTE FOR THE ADVANCEMENT OF LITERATURE, SCIENCE, AND ART

STATE OF TEXAS
COUNTY OF HARRIS
KNOW ALL MEN BY THESE PRESENTS: That F. A. Rice, James A. Baker, Jr., E. Raphael, C. Lombardi, J. E. McAshan and A. S. Richardson, residents of the City of Houston, State of Texas, availing themselves of the rights, benefits, immunities, powers and privileges conferred by an Act of the Legislature of the State of Texas, entitled: "An Act concerning private Corporations," approved April 23rd, 1874, Article 565, of the Revised Statutes of Texas, do for themselves and their successors, hereby create and establish a body politic and corporate under the name of the WILLIAM M. RICE INSTITUTE FOR THE ADVANCEMENT OF LITERATURE, SCIENCE, AND ART, for the purposes and objects, and in the manner mentioned in the following Articles:

ARTICLE ONE (1)

This Institution shall have the power to enjoy and have succession by its corporate name, for the period of fifty (50) years; to contract and be contracted with; to sue and be sued in its corporate name; to make and use a corporate seal; to receive, hold, and enjoy property, real, personal and mixed, and to rent, loan, lease or sell the same, for the uses and benefits of the Institution in such manner as in the judgment of the Board of Trustees may be best for the interests of the Institution; to have and appoint such Trustees, Managers, or Officers, and to make such By-Laws as its interest and convenience may require, and to do and perform all other things necessary to carry into effect the objects and purposes of this Corporation.

ARTICLE TWO (2)

The objects, intents, and purposes of this Institution are declared to be the establishment and maintenance, in the City of Houston, Texas, of a Public Library, and the maintenance of an Institution for the Advancement of Literature, Science, Art, Philosophy and Letters; the establishment and maintenance of a Polytechnic school; for procuring and maintaining scientific collections; collections of chemical and philosophical apparatus, me-

151

chanical and artistic models, drawings, pictures and statues; and for cultivating other means of instruction for the white inhabitants of the City of Houston, and State of Texas, to, for, and upon the uses, intents, and purposes, and upon the trusts, and subject to the conditions and restrictions contained in a deed which is in form, substance and words as follows, that is to say:

THE STATE OF TEXAS
COUNTY OF HARRIS

This INDENTURE made and entered into the thirteenth day of May, in the year Eighteen Hundred and Ninety-One, by and between William M. Rice, of the City and State of New York, party of the first part, and James A. Baker, Jr. E. Raphael, C. Lombardi, J. E. McAshan, F. A. Rice, and A. S. Richardson, of the City of Houston, County of Harris, and State of Texas, parties hereunto of the second part, WITNESSETH:

That the party of the first part, for and in consideration of the sum of One Dollar to him paid by the said parties hereto of the second part, the receipt whereof is hereby acknowledged, and of other good considerations to him thereunto moving, has given, granted, delivered and conveyed, and by these presents doth give, grant, deliver, and convey unto the said parties of the second part, and to their successors, as hereinafter provided, the sum of Two Hundred Thousand Dollars, as evidenced by the certain promissory note executed by the said party of the first part and delivered by him unto the said parties of the second part, and of which the following is a substantial copy, to-wit;

Houston, Texas, May 13th, 1891

$200,000

At my death, for value received, I promise to pay, in Houston, Harris County, Texas, to the order of F. A. Rice, Jas. A. Baker, Jr. E. Raphael, C. Lombardi, J. E. Mc Ashan and A. S. Richardson, for the "William M. Rice Institute for the advancement of Literature, Science and Art" (to be incorporated) the sum of Two Hundred Thousand Dollars, with interest at the rate of two and one half per cent per annum until paid; interest payable annually. This note is made in conformity with the terms of a certain deed of Donation this day executed and delivered by me to the said F. A. Rice, Jas. A. Baker, Jr. E. Raphael, C. Lombardi, J. E. Mc Ashan and A. S. Richardson, trustees for the use and benefit of the "William M. Rice Institute for the advancement of Literature, Science, and Art" (to be incorporated).

(Signed) W. M. Rice.

TO HAVE AND TO HOLD the said above mentioned Two Hundred Thousand Dollars, together with the interest, issues, incomes and profits thereof unto the said parties of the second part, and their successors; in trust, nevertheless, and subject to the following conditions and restrictions to, for, and upon the following uses, intents, and purposes, to-wit:

FIRST: That the above sum of Two Hundred Thousand Dollars is an Endowment Fund; that the interest, incomes, issues and profits thereof shall forever be devoted to the instruction and improvement of the white inhabitants of the City of Houston, and State of Texas, through and by the establishment and maintenance of a Public Library and Institute for the advancement of Literature, Science and Art, to be incorporated as hereinafter provided, and to be known by such name as the said parties of the second part, may in their judgment select.

SECOND: That the parties of the second part, shall forthwith proceed to incorporate themselves under the General Incorporation Laws of the State of Texas, into a body politic for the purpose of carrying out the uses, intents, and purposes of this Trust.

THIRD: That as soon as the said Public Library and Institute for the advancement of Science and Art shall have been incorporated, as herein contemplated, then the said Institute, through and by its Board of Trustees hereinafter named, shall accept from the said parties of the second part, the Endowment Fund of Two Hundred Thousand Dollars.

FOURTH: The Articles of Incorporation hereinbefore referred to shall provide for seven Trustees, and the names and residences of those first appointed shall be:

William M. Rice,	New York City.
F. A. Rice	Houston, Texas.
James A. Baker, Jr.	Houston, Texas.
E. Raphael	Houston, Texas.
C. Lombardi	Houston, Texas.
J. E. Mc Ashan	Houston, Texas.
A. S. Richardson	Houston, Texas.

The members of such Board of Trustees shall hold their Offices, as such, for life. Should any vacancy in the Board of Trustees occur by death, resignation or removal, during the life of the party of the first part, then he reserves the right to fill such vacancy. After the death of the party of the first part any vacancy in the Board of Trustees shall be filled by a vote of the surviving Trustees, taken by ballot, and it shall require at least four votes to elect such Trustee.

Any Trustee who may be elected or appointed hereafter to fill a vancancy in the Board of Trustees, shall be an inhabitant of the City of Houston, Texas.

FIFTH: The party of the first part reserves the right, during his natural life, to direct and control, by the advice and with the assistance of the Board of Trustees, the investment of the Endowment Fund, with the increase and profits thereof, and the management of the said Institute. Should, however, there at any time be a difference of opinion, between the party of the first part and said Trustees as to the investment or expenditures of said funds, or the management of said Institute, then the decision of the said party of the first part shall control.

SIXTH: Upon the death of the party of the first part it is his desire, and he so directs, that the entire control and management of the said Endowment Fund, and such other endowments, donations and bequests, as may be added thereto, together with the increase and profits thereof shall be in the hands, and under the direction of said Trustees and their successors.

SEVENTH: The Endowment Fund, herein mentioned, including all future endowments, donations, and bequests that may hereafter be made to the said Institute, not otherwise provided, shall be devoted to the following objects and purposes, to-wit;

A. To the establishment and maintenance of a Free Library, Reading-room, and Institute for the Advancement of Science and Art.

B. To provide, as soon as the fund will warrant, such an expenditure, for the establishment and maintenance of a thorough polytechnic school, for males and females, designed to give instructions on the application of science and Art to the useful occupations of life; the requirements for admission to which shall be left to the discretion of the Board of Trustees.

C. Said Library, Reading Room, Scientific Department, and Polytechnic School, and the instruction, benefits and enjoyments to be derived from the Institute to be free and open to all; to be non-sectarian and non-partisan, and subject to such restrictions only, as in the judgment of the Board of Trustees will conduce to the good order and honor of the said Institute.

EIGHTH: Said Institute, when chartered, and in operation, shall be subject to the visitation of any Courts of Justice which are now, or hereafter may be thereunto empowered, for the purpose of preventing and redressing any mismanagement, waste, or breach of trust.

NINTH: The Trustees of said Institute, are hereby expressly forbidden ever to permit any lien, encumbrance, debt or mortgage to be placed upon any of the property, or funds, belonging now, or that may hereafter belong to the said Institute; and it is the desire of the party of the first part, and he so directs, that the entire property of the Institute shall always be kept free from debt.

TENTH: The Trustees shall not receive any compensation for their services. A member of the Board of Trustees may, for sufficient cause be removed, but such removal shall not take place except by a two-thirds vote of the Board.

ELEVENTH: Full authority is hereby given to said Trustees to formulate and enforce such By-laws, rules, and regulations, for the government of the affairs of said Institute as in their judgment they may deem proper.

TWELFTH: The said Board of Trustees shall publish each year, in the month of May, beginning in May, 189   an Annual Account, under oath, of all the Receipts and Expenditures of the aforesaid Institute.

THIRTEENTH: It is expressly provided that one tenth of the increase of the Endowment Fund, herein mentioned, shall be set apart as a Sinking Fund which may be used in the discretion of the Board of Trustees for betterments and improvements of the Institute.

IN WITNESS WHEREOF, the said parties hereto have hereunto set their hands in the City of Houston the day and year first above written.

W. M. Rice

F. A. Rice

Jas. A. Baker, Jr.

E. Raphael

C. Lombardi

J. E. Mc Ashan

A. S. Richardson

(SEAL)

THE STATE OF TEXAS
COUNTY OF HARRIS

Before me, C. W. Bocock, a Notary Public in and for said County and State, on this day personally appeared W. M. Rice, F. A. Rice, Jas. A. Baker, Jr., E. Raphael, C. Lombardi, J. E. Mc Ashan and A. S. Richardson, known to me to be the persons whose names are subscribed to the foregoing instruement [sic], and severally acknowledged to me that they executed the same for the purposes and considerations therein expressed.

Given under my hand and seal of Office, this 16th day of May, A. D. 1891.

C. W. Bocock,

Notary Public, Harris County, Texas.

(SEAL)

ARTICLE THREE (3)

The office of the said Institute shall be established and remain in the City of Houston, State of Texas.

ARTICLE FOUR (4)

The period for which this Institute is to exist shall be fifty years.

ARTICLE FIVE (5)

The corporate powers of this Institute shall be managed and exercised by a Board of Seven Trustees, and the names and residences of those first appointed are as follows: to-wit:

William M. Rice	New York City.
F. A. Rice	Houston, Texas.
James A. Baker, Jr.	Houston, Texas.
E. Raphael	Houston, Texas.
C. Lombardi	Houston, Texas.
J. E. Mc Ashan	Houston, Texas.
A. S. Richardson	Houston, Texas.

ARTICLE SIX (6)

The corporation hereby created is authorized and empowered to execute the Trusts and powers mentioned in and intended to be created by the aforesaid deed set forth in Article Two (2) hereof; to accept such deed, and to hold the endowment therein mentioned with the increase and profits thereof, including all endowments, donations, and bequests at any time to be made to the said Institute, subject to the conditions and restrictions created in said deed, and to, for and upon the uses, intents, and purposes therein expressed and provided.

ARTICLE SEVEN (7)

The Corporation hereby created, and the Board of Trustees thereof, are hereby authorized and empowered to do and perform all and every act and thing whatever, and to carry out and accomplish all and every trust, intent, and purpose provided to be done, carried out or accomplished, in and by the aforesaid deed in respect to the said Corporation or Board of Trustees; and the said Corporation is hereby also authorized and empowered to receive all and every endowment, .donation and bequest made to it, and to appropriate the same to the uses, intents, and purposes contemplated herein and in said deed.

ARTICLE EIGHT (8)

The said Insititute has no Capital stock.

WITNESS our hands at Houston, Texas, this the 18th day of May, A. D. 1891.

F. A. Rice
Jas. A. Baker Jr.
E. Raphael
C. Lombardi
J E McAshan
A S Richardson

NOTE: The foregoing instrument was acknowledged before C. W. Bocock, Notary Public, Harris County, 18 May 1891 and filed 19 May 1891, Department of State, endorsed by Geo. W. Smith, Secretary of State. Charters of Incorporation (MS in Secretary of State's Office, Austin, Texas), file 5095. Endorsement shows file box 102, K-600. With typographical errors, printed, from certified copy certified 11 December 1900, by Geo. T. Keeble, chief clerk and acting secretary of state, in In the Matter of the Probate of the Last Will and Testament of William M. Rice, deceased, as a Will of Real and Personal Property (Instrument bearing date September 26, 1896), record on appeal, II, 851-860.

At special meeting 23 April 1941 resolution of Board of Trustees to extend charter under Article 1315 (a) of States of Texas, as amended, 50 years from and after 18 May 1941, with all privileges, powers, immunities, rights of succession of original charter. B. B. Rice, Secretary, 23 April 1941. Acknowledged 26 April 1941, before Inez Buvens, Notary Public, Harris County. Financial statement, 30 June 1940: Assets $17,942,863.35. $10 filing fee, extension 50 years. Filed 28 April 1941. Charters of Incorporation, file 5095.

ELIZABETH BALDWIN RICE'S CONTESTED WILL
(June 1, 1896)

KNOW ALL MEN BY THESE PRESENTS, that I, Elizabeth B. Rice, of the County of Harris, State of Texas, being in good health and of sound and disposing mind and memory, do make and publish this my last will and testament, hereby revoking all other wills or papers by me at any time made.

First. I direct that all my just debts shall be paid, and that the legacies hereinafter given shall, after the payment of my debts, be paid out of my estate.

Second. I give to my sister Mrs. J. Sales Brown of Los Angeles, California, the sum of Fifty thousand dollars, for her use and benefit.

Third. I give to my sister Bettie B. Brown of Los Angeles, California, the sum of Fifty thousand dollars.

Fourth. I give to Mamie B. Huntington of Cleveland, Ohio, the sum of Two hundred thousand dollars.

Fifth. I give to Lillian E. Huntington, the daughter of Mamie B. Huntington, the sum of One hundred thousand dollars.

Sixth. I give to my brother Jonas C. Baldwin the sum of Fifty thousand dollars for his use, during his natural life, and at his death the same shall divert and pass to his daughter Mamie B. Huntington.

Seventh. I give and bequeath to the child or children of Henry and Minnie R. Lummis, of Houston, Texas, the sum of Twenty-five thousand dollars to be used equally for them and in the case of the death of said child or children the then said sum shall revert to their mother Minnie R. Lummis.

Eighth. I give and bequeath to my second cousin Miss Adele Baldwin of the State of New York, the sum of Twenty-five thousand dollars for her own use.

Ninth. I give to Marian Roberts of Brooklyn, N. Y., daughter of Julia & Jacob Roberts the sum of Twenty-five thousand dollars.

Tenth. I give to Julia Roberts of the State of New York, the sum of Twenty-five thousand dollars.

Eleventh. I give to Lola Morton of New York, State of New York, the sum of Twenty-five thousand dollars.

Twelfth. I give to Isabella Dorwin daughter of Thomas Dorwin of Syracuse, N.Y., the sum of Twenty-five thousand dollars.

Thirteenth. I give to Annie G. Lippincott, daughter of Grace Greenwood of Washington, D. C., the sum of Twenty-five thousand dollars.

Fourteenth. I give to the children of David & Mattie Rice of Houston, Texas, the sum of Fifty thousand dollars.

Fifteenth. I give to Stephen W. Baldwin of the State of New York of Baldwinsville, the sum of Twelve thousand five hundred dollars.

Sixteenth. I give to Frank M. Baldwin of Baldwinsville, N. Y. the sum of Twelve thousand five hundred dollars.

Seventeenth. I give to the son of Stephen W. Baldwin of Baldwinsville, N. Y. the sum of Twelve thousand five hundred dollars.

Eighteenth. I give to Sarah Baldwin of Baldwinsville, N. Y. the daughter of I. M. Baldwin, the sum of twelve thousand five hundred dollars.

Nineteenth. I give to my cousin Belle Wallace, daughter of Jonas C. Wallace the sum of Twelve thousand five hundred dollars.

Twentieth. I give and bequeath to Miss Bessie Campbell of Houston, Texas, the sum of Five thousand dollars.

Twentyfirst. I give to Dr. R. Rutherford of Houston, the sum of Twenty-five thousand dollars.

Twentysecond. I give to Mrs. Heriot of Los Angeles, California, the sum of Five thousand dollars.

Twentythird. It is my desire to erect a home to my memory in Baldwinsville, State of New York, to be given as a home for indigent gentlewomen and to be called and known as The Elizabeth Baldwin Home. It is to be located and situated in the town of Baldwinsville, State of New York, and I desire to be purchased what is known as "The Old Wallace Homestead" Baldwinsville, N. Y., if the same can be purchased for a reasonable price and if not, some other site, in the said town of Baldwinsville N. Y. on which to erect the said home, said home to be conducted and managed as near as may be to the Louise Home in Washington, D. C. (Louise Home founded by Corcoran). I hereby appoint as trustees and desire they carry out my plans, to manage and conduct said home, Stephen W. Baldwin and Frank M. Baldwin of Baldwinsville, N. Y., and I hereby give and bequeath to the said trustees, the sum of Two hundred and fifty thousand dollars to be used exclusively by the said trustees with which to build and maintain said home and erect the same as above indicated. I desire and direct that One hundred thousand dollars be used in the purchase of land and erecting a building thereon, and that One hundred and fifty thousand dollars be invested in good securities, the proceeds of which shall be used to maintain and support said home; and in case one or both of said trustees should resign, die, or refuse to act, then the Governor of the State of New York, is empowered and directed to appoint successors to said trustee or trustees, who shall have all the power and authority given to the trustees by the terms of this will. It is my desire and I so direct, that the said trustees keep an account accurate and correct and a statement of all monies expended by them and file such statement with the Probate or Surrogate Court of the County in which said home is situated.

Twentyfourth. I desire to have purchased within the corporate limits of the City of Houston, Texas, a tract of land for a park and to have the same improved and beautified, and the same is to be known as The Elizabeth Baldwin Park, and I hereby direct and give to my executor the sum of One hundred thousand dollars to be expended by him in purchasing and improving and beautifying said park, which is to be used by the public, and in said park the said executor is directed to erect a fountain to be known as The Charlotte Allen Fountain, which is to cost not exceeding Five thousand dollars.

Twentyfifth. I give to the Parish Aid Society of Christ Church, Houston, Texas, the sum of Five thousand dollars, to be used by said society as they see proper.

Twentysixth. I give to the Faith Home of Houston, Texas, the sum of Five thousand dollars.

Twentyseventh. I give to the Bayland Orphans Home, Houston, Texas, the sum of Five thousand dollars.

Twentyeighth. I give to the First Presbyterian Church of Houston, Texas, the sum of Five thousand dollars.

Twentyninth. I give to Christ Church Episcopal, the sum of Twenty thousand dollars, said church known as Christ Church is situated on the corner of Texas Avenue and Fannin Street, Houston, Texas.

Thirtieth. I give and bequeath to the Society of New York known as the Drawing Room Society, of which I am a member, the sum of Five thousand dollars.

Thirty-One. I give to the Diet Kitchen Society of which I am a member, the sum of Five thousand dollars, said Diet Kitchen is located in New York

City.

Thirtysecond. I give and bequeath all my jewels and laces to my niece Mamie B. Huntington of Cleveland, Ohio.

Thirtythird. I desire and so direct my executor to invest Five thousand dollars, and to use the proceeds thereof to keep my, or our lot in Glenwood Cemetery in Houston, Texas, in good order.

Thirtyfourth. I desire and direct that pictures of my beloved husband William M. Rice and my aunt, Charlotte Allen be purchased and placed in the William M. Rice Library Building, Houston, Texas, and that my executor purchase the said pictures and I appropriate not exceeding Fifteen thousand dollars therefor.

Thirtyfifth. In case my estate after my death is sufficient in amount, then I desire to double all the personal bequests except Dr. R. Rutherford of Houston, Texas. This is not intended to double any bequest to any institutions or societies, but only applies to natural persons, then I desire to increase each and all of said personal bequests as far as my estate will do so.

Thirtysixth. It is my desire after my death to be buried in Glenwood Cemetery Houston, Texas and have erected over my grave a suitable and appropriate monument, with the proper inscriptions thereon, the monument to cost not less than Five thousand dollars. I desire such amount set aside for such purpose.

Thirtyseventh. I do solemnly declare that if I signed any papers at any time, giving away or willing away any of my property, I did so without knowing their purpose and so declare them void. I signed some papers giving the Louisiana lands away and knew what they were for, There were other papers which were not read to me. Those I declare to be of no good as I did not wish at any time of my life to sign away my rights in my part of the property, either real or personal, and I direct and instruct my executor to examine all such papers, and if he has reason to believe that they were signed without my full knowledge and consent, and knowing what they were, he is to declare them illegal and act as he thinks best. And I trust my husband William M. Rice will give no trouble to my executor in regard to my will, as I have considered this writing of my will for many months.

Thirtyeighth. I constitute and appoint O. T. Holt of Houston, Texas sole executor of this, my last will and I desire as compensation to him for his services, that he receive as his just due ten per cent of all amount received and paid out by him under the terms of this will, and in case there is any litigation, I desire my said executor to bring suit or defend any suit involving any of my property, or the construction of this will and for such services he shall receive additional reasonable compensation.

Thirtyninth. In case I receive at my death any real or personal property, then I direct my executor to sell and dispose of all such real and personal property and convert same into money and use the same in paying off the bequests and carrying out the terms of this will, and in case I die possessed of real and personal property my executor is hereby authorized to pay off and discharge all said legacies with such real and personal property, the same as if it were cash.

Fortieth. I direct that no security or bond shall be required of my executor.

Forty-One. It is my will that no other action shall be had in the County Court in the administration of my estate, than to prove and record this will and to return an inventory and appraisement of my estate and list of claims, and I authorize and empower my said executor to sell and dispose of any portion of my estate, real or personal at public or private sale in a manner that may to him seem best for the purpose of paying my just debts and the legacies herein bequeathed.

In witness whereof I set my Hand this the first day of June 1896 in the presence of Laura J. Seward and Anna Wallace who attest the same at my request.

(signed) Elizabeth B. Rice

The above instrument was now here subscribed by Elizabeth B. Rice, the testatrix in our presence and we at her request and in her presence, sign our names hereto as attesting witnesses.

(signed) Laura J. Seward
Anna Wallace

WILLIAM MARSH RICE'S WILL
(September 26, 1896)

The State of New York
County and City of New York.

I, William M. Rice, of the City, County, and State of New York, do make and publish, this, my last will and testament, hereby revoking, any, and all other wills, heretofore, made by me.

First. It is my desire, and I so direct, that all of my just debts shall be paid by my executors, hereinafter named, the survivors or survivor of them, as soon after my death as, by them, may be found convenient.

Second. I give, devise and bequeath to my executors, hereinafter named, the survivors, or survivor of them, the sum of Eighty thousand Dollars, for the use and benefit of my brother, Frederick A. Rice, and his wife Charlotte. It is my desire, and I so direct, that said sum of money shall be invested, by my said executors, the survivors or survivor of them, in such manner and in such securities as, in their judgment, will yield the largest returns consistent with safety of investment; and the income thereof shall be paid, annually, by my executors, the survivors or survivor of them, to my said brother Frederick A. Rice, and his wife Charlotte, for their maintenance and support, during their respective lives. In the event of the death of either of them, then, said income shall be paid to the survivor during his or her lifetime. The surplus of said income, if any, may be paid by said Frederick A. Rice and his wife, Charlotte, if they so elect, or the survivor of them, if he or she so elect, to J. S. Rice, F. A. Rice Jr, David Rice, George Rice, Minnie Lummis, wife of H. H. Lummis, and Libbie Timpson wife of Paul B. Timpson, any or all of them, in such proportions as the said Frederick A. Rice and his wife, Charlotte, or the survivor of them, may deem best. After the death of said Frederick A. Rice and his wife Charlotte, it is my desire, and I so direct that my executors, the survivors or survivor of them, shall pay said sum of Eighty thousand Dollars to the surviving above mentioned children of F. A. Rice and his wife Charlotte.

Third. I give, devise and bequeath to my executors hereinafter named, the survivors or survivor of them, the sum of Ten thousand Dollars for the use and benefit of my sister, Minerva R. Olds, of the State of Massachusetts. It is my desire, and I so direct, that said sum of money shall be invested by my said executors, the survivors or survivor of them, in such manner and in such securities as, in their judgment, will yield the largest returns consistent with safety of investment; and the income thereof shall be paid, annually, by my executors, the survivors or survivor of them, to my said sister, Minerva R. Olds, for her maintenance and support during her lifetime. Upon the death of my said sister, Minerva R. Olds, I give, devise, and bequeath said sum of Ten Thousand Dollars to her daughters, and my executors, the survivors or survivor of them, are directed, upon her death, to pay said sum of Ten thousand Dollars to said daughters.

Fourth. I give, devise and bequeath to my executors hereinafter named the survivors or survivor of them, the sum of Ten Thousand Dollars for the use and benefit of my sister, Charlotte S. McKee, of the State of Massachusetts. It is my desire, and I so direct, that said sum of Ten Thousand Dollars shall be invested by my said executors, the survivors or survivor of them, in such manner and in such securities as, in their judgment, will yield the largest returns consistent with safety of investment; and the income thereof shall be paid, annually, by my executors, the survivors, or survivor of them, to my said sister, Charlotte S. McKee, for her maintenance and support during her lifetime. Upon the death of my said sister, Charlotte S. McKee, I give, devise and bequeath said sum of Ten Thousand Dollars to her daughters and daughter in law, and my executors, the survivors or survivor of them, are directed, upon the death of my said sister, Charlotte S. McKee, to pay said sum of Ten thousand Dollars to said Daughters and Daughter in law the wife of her son.

Fifth. I give, devise and bequeath to my nephew, William M. Rice Jr, of the State of Texas, all of the indebtedness of every kind that may be due, at my death, to my estate, by the firm of J. I. and W. M. Rice, of Hyatt, Texas.

Sixth. All the rest and residue of my estate, real, personal and mixed, and wheresoever situate, I give, devise and bequeath unto the "William M. Rice Institute for the advancement of Literature, Science and Art," a corporation domiciled in the City of Houston, in Harris County, Texas.

Seventh. It is my desire that my namesake, William M. Rice Jr, shall be elected to fill the vacancy in the Board of Directors of the "William M. Rice Institute, for the advancement of Literature, Science and Art," caused by my death; and I express the hope that he will take an interest in the prosperity and success of said Institute, and that he will continue to act as a member of said Directory.

Eighth. It is my desire, and I so direct that my friend, Mr. E. Raphael, of Houston, Texas, shall act in the capacity of Secretary of the "William M. Rice Institute, for the advancement of Literature, Science and Art," and I hope he will continue to act in said capacity as long as he wishes, and feels an interest in the success of the purposes for which said Institute was formed. It is my desire that he shall be paid from the income of said Institute fair and reasonable compensation for his services performed and to be performed as such Secretary. It is not intended by this provision of my will that the said Raphael shall be continued as Secretary of said Institute if, in the judgment of the Board of Directors thereof, some other should be appointed.

Ninth: I nominate, constitute and appoint my nephew, William M. Rice, Jr, of the State of Texas, John D. Bartine of New Jersey, and James A. Baker Jr of Houston Texas, the survivors or survivor of them, executors of this my last will and testament; and it is my desire, and I so direct, that no bond, or other security, shall ever be required of my executors, the survivors or survivor of them, as such executors. In the event of the death of any of said executors, or in case of the failure or refusal of any of them to act as such executors, then the survivors or survivor of them, shall act and shall be invested with all the rights, powers and duties granted to all of said executors.

Tenth. It is my desire, and I so direct that my executors herein mentioned, the survivors or survivor of them, for the services to be performed by them as such, shall receive a commission of five per cent upon the aggregate value of the whole of my Estate.

Eleventh. In the event any differences shall arise, at any time, between my executors, as to the management of my Estate, then if there are more than two directors acting, the judgment of a majority of them shall control. If there are only two executors acting, then in the event of differences between them, in the management of the Estate, the judgment and decision of   shall control.

Twelfth. It is my desire and I so direct that no other action shall be had in any probate court in reference to the administration of my estate further than to probate and establish this will, and to return an inventory and appraisement of my estate.

Thirteenth. For the purpose of carrying out the objects and intent of this will, paying debts, and realizing the cash money bequeathed and devised to my executors for the use and benefit of Frederick A. Rice and his wife Charlotte, and my sisters, Minerva R. Olds and Charlotte S. McKee, full and ample power and authority are hereby given to my executors, the survivors or survivor of them, to sell such of my estate as they may think best.

In testimony whereof I have hereunto signed my name to this instrument, in the presence of W. O. Wetherbee and W. F. Harmon, as subscribing witnesses, who sign the same at my request, in my presence and in the presence of each other this the 26th day of September 1896.

W. M. RICE   (Seal)

Signed, sealed, published and declared by the said testator as and for his last will and testament in our presence, who at his request, in his presence, and in the presence of each other have hereunto subscribed our names as attesting witnesses this the 26th day of September 1896.

| W. O. Wetherbee | Residing 300 Greene Avenue | Brooklyn N. Y. |
| W. F. Harmon | ”   672 Putnam Ave | Brooklyn N. Y. |

THE FORGED OR PATRICK WILL
(June 30, 1900)

THE STATE, CITY AND   )

                  : SS.:

COUNTY OF NEW YORK.   )

        BE IT KNOWN, that I, W I L L I A M M. R I C E, being of sound and disposing mind and memory, hereby revoking any and all other wills heretofore by me made, do hereby make, publish and declare this, my last will and testament, as follows, that is to say:

First: I nominate, constitute and appoint my nephew William M. Rice, Jr., of Hyatt, Texas; James A. Baker, Jr, of Houston, Texas and Albert T. Patrick, of New York, the survivors or survivor of them, as and to be the executors of this my Last Will and Testament; and I will and direct that no bond or other security shall ever be required of them as such executors; that for the services performed by them as such executors, they shall receive a commission of five per cent (5%) upon the aggregate value of the whole of my estate, coming into their possession as such executors, excluding such gifts from me to the William M. Rice Institute hereinafter mentioned as may be vested otherwise than by this will; that no other action shall be had in any Probate Court in reference to the administration of my estate than to probate and establish this Will and to return an inventory and appraisement of my estate, except as is otherwise required by law, and that, for the purpose of paying debts and carrying out the provisions of this Will, full power and authority is hereby given to my said executors, the survivors or survivor of them, to sell any and all of my estate, real, personal or mixed, as they may deem best.

Second: I give, devise and bequeath unto the "William M. Rice Institute for the Advancement of Literature, Science and Art", a corporation under the laws of the State of Texas, a sufficient sum of money, which together with and inclusive of the vested gifts, real, personal or mixed, heretofore or hereafter in my lifetime made by me to the said Institute, will amount in value to the sum of two hundred and fifty thousand dollars ($250,000) provided that if the vested gifts, real, personal or mixed, heretofore or hereafter made by me in my lifetime to said Institute shall, at the time of my death, equal to or exceed in value the sum of two hundred and fifty thousand

169

dollars ($250,000), then this legacy is to be null and void.

Third: I give and bequeath to my brother, Frederick A. Rice or to his lineal heirs, per stirpes, if he die before me, the sum of fifty thousand dollars ($50,000).

Fourth: I give, devise and bequeath the sum of twenty-five thousand dollars ($25,000) to each of my brothers and sisters, surviving me at the time of my death, and also to the lineal heirs, if any, per stirpes, of each of my predeceased brothers and sisters.

Fifth: I give and bequeath the sum of five thousand dollars ($5,000) to each of my nephews and nieces surviving me at the time of my death, and also to the lineal heirs, if any, per stirpes, of each of my pre-deceased nephews and nieces.

Sixth: I give and bequeath to each of the persons who at the time of my death may be directors of the said "William M. Rice Institute for the Advancement of Literature, Science and Art", the sum of five thousand dollars ($5,000) for which I desire and expect them to manifest an interest in said Institute all their lives.

Seventh: I give and bequeath the sum of five thousand dollars ($5,000) to each of the following named persons, that is to say: Charles T. Adams, of Montclair, N.J.; A. B. Cohn, of Houston, Texas; John D. Bartine, of Somerville, N. J.; and W. O. Wetherbee, of New York; and also to Frederick L. Blinn, of Springfield, Mass., if he does not otherwise take under my will.

Eighth: I give and bequeath the sum of one thousand dollars ($1,000) to each of the following named persons, that is to say: William Rice Carpenter, of Dunnellen, N. J.; Mrs. John W. Boothby, W. F. Harmon and John H. Wallace of New York.

Ninth: I give and bequeath the sum of five hundred dollars ($500) to each of the following named persons, that is to say: Charles Carpenter, his wife Isabel Carpenter of Dunnellen, N. J.; W. G. Rucker of Groesbeck, Texas; John E. Matheson, William Dale and Paul Teisch, of New York.

Tenth: The foregoing provisions of my Will are upon the express condition precedent that the above mentioned legatees, respectively, will accept, without contest in the Courts or otherwise all the conditions hereof, and that they will execute such conveyances and release of any and all of my estate wheresoever situated and of whatsoever nature, to the said Albert T. Patrick, as he may demand; and any legatee not so doing is forever debarred from taking under this Will or in any manner inheriting any portion of my estate, and such portion shall enure to the said Albert T. Patrick.

Eleventh: I give, devise and bequeath to Albert T. Patrick, formerly of Texas, now of New York, all the rest and residue of my estate, real, personal and mixed, heretofore or hereafter acquired and wheresoever situated.

IN TESTIMONY WHEREOF, I, the said William M. Rice, to this my Last Will and Testament, have subscribed my name and affixed my seal in the presence of Morris Meyers and David L. Short as subscribing witnesses, who sign the same as subscribing witnesses at my request, in my presence and in the presence of each other this 30 day of June, A.D. nineteen hundred (1900).

W. M. Rice   (Seal)

Signed, sealed, published and declared by the said William M. Rice, as, for and to be his last Will and Testament, in our presence, and we, at his request and in his presence and in the presence of each other, have hereunto signed our names as witnesses this 30 day of June A.D. nineteen hundred (1900).

Name.	*Occupation.*	*Address.*
Morris Meyers	Lawyer	168 Henry St. Manhattan N.Y. City
David L. Short	Publisher	404 Bradford St. Brooklyn, N.Y.